A Note From Rick Renner

I am on a personal quest to see a "revival of the Bible" so people can establish their lives on a firm foundation that will stand strong and endure the test as end-time storm winds begin to intensify.

In order to experience a revival of the Bible in your personal life, it is important to take time each day to read, receive, and apply its truths to your life. James tells us that if we will continue in the perfect law of liberty — refusing to be forgetful hearers, but determined to be doers — we will be blessed in our ways. As you watch or listen to the programs in this series and work through this corresponding study guide, I trust you will search the Scriptures and allow the Holy Spirit to help you hear something new from God's Word that applies specifically to your life. I encourage you to be a doer of the Word He reveals to you. Whatever the cost, I assure you — it will be worth it.

> Thy words were found, and I did eat them;
> and thy word was unto me the joy and rejoicing of mine heart:
> for I am called by thy name, O Lord God of hosts.
> — Jeremiah 15:16

Your brother and friend in Jesus Christ,

Rick Renner

Unless otherwise indicated, all scripture quotations are taken from the *King James Version* of the Bible.

Scripture quotations marked (*AMPC*) are taken from the *Amplified® Bible*. Copyright © 1954, 1958, 1962, 1964, 1965, 1987 by The Lockman Foundation. Used by permission. **www.Lockman.org**.

Scriptures marked as (*GNT*) are taken from the **Good News Translation - Second Edition** © 1992 by American Bible Society. Used by permission.

Scripture quotations marked (*MSG*) are taken from *The Message*, copyright © 1993, 2002, 2018 by Eugene H. Peterson. Used by permission of NavPress. All rights reserved. Represented by Tyndale House Publishers, Inc.

Scripture quotations taken from the New American Standard Bible® (*NASB*) copyright © 1960, 1962, 1963, 1968, 1971, 1972, 1973, 1975, 1977, 1995 by The Lockman Foundation. Used by permission. **www.Lockman.org**.

Scripture quotations marked (*NLT*) are taken from the Holy Bible, *New Living Translation*, copyright © 1996, 2004, 2015 by Tyndale House Foundation. Used by permission of Tyndale House Publishers, Inc., Carol Stream, Illinois 60188. All rights reserved.

Scripture quotations marked *RIV* are taken from *Renner Interpretive Version*. Copyright © 2021 by Rick Renner.

The Apostles' Creed

Copyright © 2023 by Rick Renner
1814 W. Tacoma St.
Broken Arrow, OK 74012-1406

Published by Rick Renner Ministries
www.renner.org

ISBN 13: 978-1-6675-0358-5

eBook ISBN 13: 978-1-6675-0359-2

All rights reserved. No portion of this book may be reproduced or transmitted in any form or by any means — electronic, mechanical, photocopy, recording, scanning, or other — except for brief quotations in critical reviews or articles, without the prior written permission of the Publisher.

How To Use This Study Guide

This 15-lesson study guide corresponds to *"The Apostles' Creed" With Rick Renner* (Renner TV). Each lesson in this study guide covers a topic that is addressed during the program series, with questions and references supplied to draw you deeper into your own private study of the Scriptures on this subject.

To derive the most benefit from this study guide, consider the following:

First, watch or listen to the program prior to working through the corresponding lesson in this guide. (Programs can also be viewed at **renner.org** by clicking on the Media/Archives links or on our Renner Ministries YouTube channel.)

Second, take the time to look up the scriptures included in each lesson. Prayerfully consider their application to your own life.

Third, use a journal or notebook to make note of your answers to each lesson's Study Questions and Practical Application challenges.

Fourth, invest specific time in prayer and in the Word of God to consult with the Holy Spirit. Write down the scriptures or insights He reveals to you.

Finally, take action! Whatever the Lord tells you to do according to His Word, do it.

For added insights on this subject, it is recommended that you obtain Rick Renner's books *Paid in Full: An In-depth Look at the Defining Moments of Christ's Passion, Build Your Foundation: Six Must-Have Beliefs for Constructing an Unshakable Christian Life,* and *How To Keep Your Head on Straight in a World Gone Crazy.* You may also select from Rick's other available resources by placing your order at **renner.org** or by calling 1-800-742-5593.

LESSON 1

TOPIC
God the Father, Creator of Heaven and Earth

SCRIPTURES
1. **Ephesians 3:20** — Now unto him that is able to do exceeding abundantly above all that we ask or think….
2. **Genesis 1:1** — In the beginning God created the heaven and the earth.
3. **John 1:3** — All things were made by him; and without him was not any thing made that was made.
4. **John 1:10** — He was in the world, and the world was made by him….
5. **Colossians 1:16,17** — For by him were all things created, that are in heaven, and that are in earth, visible and invisible, whether they be thrones, or dominions, or principalities, or powers: all things were created by him, and for him: and he is before all things, and by him all things consist.
6. **Psalm 100:3** — Know ye that the Lord he is God: it is he that hath made us, and not we ourselves….
7. **Psalm 14:1** — The fool hath said in his heart, There is no God….

GREEK WORDS
No Greek words were shown on the TV program.

SYNOPSIS
The 15 lessons in this study on *The Apostles' Creed* will focus on the following topics:

- God the Father, Creator of Heaven and Earth
- Jesus Christ, His Only Son
- Born of the Virgin Mary

- Suffered Under Pontius Pilate
- Crucified, Dead, and Buried
- He Descended Into Hell
- The Third Day He Rose From the Dead
- He Ascended Into Heaven
- He Sits at the Right Hand of God the Father Almighty
- He Shall Come To Judge the Living and the Dead
- I Believe in the Holy Spirit
- The Holy Catholic (Universal) Church
- The Communion of Saints
- The Forgiveness of Sin
- The Resurrection of the Body and Life Everlasting

The emphasis of this lesson:

A gradual withdrawal from the teaching of Scripture has left many believers biblically illiterate and vulnerable to the deadly effects of false doctrine. To combat scriptural error, creeds were established by Early Church leaders — The Apostles' Creed being the most memorable. It contains the core beliefs of the Christian faith, including the opening declaration: I believe in God, the Father Almighty, the Creator of heaven and earth.

The Holy Spirit Warned Us of a Spiritual Famine in the Last Days

Writing under the inspiration of the Holy Spirit, the apostle Paul prophetically pointed his finger more than 2,000 years into the future and said, "Now the Spirit speaketh expressly, that in the latter times some shall depart from the faith, giving heed to seducing spirits, and doctrines of devils" (1 Timothy 4:1).

Notice the verse begins by saying, "Now the Spirit speaks *expressly*." When we read this in the original Greek text, it indicates the Holy Spirit is speaking very strongly. We could translate this portion of the verse to say, "The Spirit speaks *categorically*..." or "The Spirit speaks *unmistakably*..." or "The Spirit speaks *emphatically*...." To be clear, Paul is not describing something that might happen. The tense is so strong here that it signifies something that will most definitely take place in the latter times.

What's going to happen? Paul said, "The Spirit speaketh *emphatically*, *categorically*, and *unmistakably* that in the latter times some shall depart from the faith…." In Greek, the words "latter times" describe *the very end of the age*. In the nautical world, the word for "latter" was used to describe *the very last port one stopped at on a voyage*. By using this word, Paul is saying, "When you have sailed to the very end of the age and there is no time left, some shall depart from the faith, giving heed to seducing spirits, and doctrines of devils."

Interestingly, Paul said, "…Some shall depart from the faith…" (1 Timothy 4:1). This phrase "shall depart from" is the Greek word *aphistemi*, which doesn't describe an outright rejection of the faith, but rather *a very slow, methodical transitioning away from what one once stood by and believed*. It is a picture of people gradually letting go of what they were believing and reaching over and embracing a new belief.

Specifically, the Bible says they shall depart from "the faith," which in Greek is *ho pistis*. The fact that it includes the definite article *ho* indicates that this is *not* faith for miracles or faith for signs and wonders. It is THE faith, which means *the clear sound teaching of Scripture*. Thus, the Holy Spirit prophesied through Paul that at the very end of the Church age, there will be people who move away from what they once believed, and the reason for their transition is because of the activity of "seducing spirits and doctrines of devils," which lure them away from the foundational teachings of the Bible.

Many Believers Are Biblically Illiterate

Look around you. This end-time departure from the faith is happening in the Church and has been happening for quite some time. Little by little, people have retreated from the solid teachings of Scripture — including many Christian leaders. This gradual backing away from sound teaching has been going on for so long that many believers today are biblically illiterate. That is, they're unfamiliar with even the most elementary doctrines of the New Testament, and this is very unfortunate.

One reason for the lack of biblical knowledge is that many pastors in the pulpit today are no longer teaching the Bible verse by verse. Although they're masterful communicators when it comes to exhorting, encouraging, and topical teaching, they're uneducated in basic biblical principles. Some just don't feel capable of verse-by-verse teaching because they've never really been educated in biblical doctrine.

Studying Scripture verse by verse is important because it forces both the teacher and the student to dig deep into the original language and culture and to really think as they examine the text. Though unpopular, verse-by-verse study also enables us to cover every single subject in the Bible, providing a well-balanced biblical education. Without solid, biblical teaching, believers often end up spiritually malnourished.

This drift from the foundation of Scripture is not a new development. A careful study of the early centuries of the Church reveals that even at its very outset, the Church was being infiltrated with seducing spirits and doctrines of demons, which were already trying to lure people away from the clear, authoritative teaching of Scripture.

Creeds Were Established for an Important Purpose

In an effort to effectively combat scriptural error, Church leaders had to come up with a solution. They began to gather at key moments in history to forge a solid, biblical foundation for the Christian faith that all believers could hold on to. These written statements were called *creeds*, and they contained the most important tenets of the Christian faith — tenets that were nonnegotiable and could not be modified.

These vital, fixed doctrines were — and still are — to be fully embraced and proclaimed by all believers as the basis of the Christian faith. They were established to bring order and put an end to the theological madness that was erupting in the Church across the Roman Empire. In fact, the creeds that were written by early Church leaders kept the Church on track for many centuries, helping them determine right and wrong doctrine.

The first known creed was called The Old Roman Creed. It was developed during the Second Century and is the earliest known creed of the Christian faith. It is an early version of what later became known as The Apostles' Creed, and it was so well known in the Early Church that even Tertullian and Irenaeus cited it in their works.

In the late Fourth Century, an early Church leader named Tyrannius Rufinus wrote a commentary on *The Old Roman Creed* where he recounted the viewpoint that the apostles originally authored this creed together after Pentecost, before leaving Jerusalem to preach elsewhere.

The Nicene Creed is another important creed. It was composed in the year 325 AD by a special gathering of bishops who met together in the city of Nicaea, which today is Iznik, Turkey. Eusebius of Caesarea, an early Christian historian, described the Council of Nicaea as: "The most eminent servants of God from all the churches that filled Europe, Africa, and Asia...."[1]

Historians tell us that approximately 300 bishops gathered in the city of Nicaea, along with many other appointed delegates. Altogether, there were about 1,800 Christian leaders that convened and wrote what they believed were the most important tenets of the Christian faith. During that time there was a surge of false doctrine concerning the divinity of Christ that was being spread about, which they felt the need to refute.

The Apostles' Creed was the third official creed. Although the version we have today dates to the year 390 AD, it is essentially a revision of The Old Roman Creed, which was written in approximately 140 AD. Early Church fathers referred to it as "the rule of faith," and it is a condensed compilation of the teachings of the apostles, which is why it was called The Apostles' Creed.

This creed covers the core beliefs of the Christian faith, and in the centuries that followed, the Early Church used it like a "truth filter" to determine what was and wasn't genuine Christian doctrine. The Apostles' Creed is still widely used and quoted in churches all over the world today. It has been found to be very helpful in encapsulating the core beliefs for many Christians, affirming what we believe. In fact, the word "creed" means *I believe*. Here is The Apostles' Creed:

I believe in God, the Father Almighty,
the Creator of heaven and earth,
and in Jesus Christ, His only Son, our Lord:
Who was conceived of the Holy Spirit,
born of the Virgin Mary,
suffered under Pontius Pilate,
was crucified, died, and was buried.

He descended into hell.

The third day He arose again from the dead.

He ascended into heaven

and sits at the right hand of God, the Father Almighty,

whence He shall come to judge the living and the dead.

I believe in the Holy Spirit,

the holy catholic [universal] church,

the communion of saints,

the forgiveness of sins,

the resurrection of the body,

and life everlasting.

Amen.

This creed of the apostles truly is a summary of what we believe in our faith as Christians. It includes most of the major Bible doctrines, which we will see as we move through the lessons in this study. Let's begin by carefully examining the opening words of this historic creed.

'I Believe in God…'

The Apostles' Creed begins with the declaration, "I believe in God.…" Why was this such an important statement with which to begin? The reason is that at the time The Apostles' Creed was written, the Roman Empire was in control, and in the Roman Empire, they believed in many gods. In fact, if you compile a list of all the various Greek and Roman gods, it would seem almost endless. Therefore, the very first statement in The Apostles' Creed states there is only one God, and it is in that One, true God alone that we put our faith.

Although this may seem like such a simple truth, today, we're living in a world that is returning to paganism where people believe in all kinds of gods and multiple ways to get to Heaven. The doctrine of the One true God in The Apostles' Creed is absolutely essential to all that we say in terms of our Christian theology, our Christian faith, and our Christian practice.

As Christians, we believe in the eternal triune God, who has revealed Himself to us as Father, Son, and Holy Spirit — **three distinct Persons** with distinct personal attributes, but without division of nature or essence or being. Examples of this teaching can be found in:

> Matthew 3:13-17; Matthew 28:18-20; John 1:1; John 14:26; John 17:3; Romans 3:30; James 2:19

'I Believe in… the Father Almighty'

The Apostles' Creed also says, "I believe in… the Father Almighty," which is so important. It is the declaration that God is Father to all those who become His children through faith in Christ Jesus. We call Him Father because Jesus taught us to do so in Luke 11:2, when He gave us the Lord's prayer. He said, "…When ye pray, say, *Our Father* which art in heaven, Hallowed be thy name. Thy kingdom come. Thy will be done, as in heaven, so in earth."

Also notice that in The Apostles' Creed He's called *the Father Almighty*, which means He has all power to do whatever is necessary — including what appears to be impossible to us. Paul brings this out clearly in Ephesians 3:20, which says, "Now unto him that is able to do exceeding abundantly above all that we ask or think, according to the power that worketh in us."

'I Believe in… the Creator of Heaven and Earth'

The third declaration — the belief that God is the Creator of Heaven and earth — is one of the most disputed truths in the world today. This belief is challenged by atheists, anti-creationists, and even by some who profess to be Christians. It is under fire in the public school system as well as in some churches. Regardless of what people say, the Bible clearly states:

> **In the beginning God created the heaven and the earth.**
> **— Genesis 1:1**

> **All things were made by him; and without him was not any thing made that was made.**
> **— John 1:3**

> **He was in the world, and the world was made by him….**
> **— John 1:10**

The fact that God is the Creator of Heaven and earth is the foundation of both the Old and New Testaments. Under the unction of the Holy Spirit, the apostle Paul echoes this same truth:

> **For by him were all things created, that are in heaven, and that are in earth, visible and invisible, whether they be thrones, or dominions, or principalities, or powers: all things were created by him, and for him: and he is before all things, and by him all things consist.**
>
> — Colossians 1:16,17

In this passage we see that not only is God the Creator, He is also the sustainer of everything that exists! Even the psalmist declares the truth that God is Creator. We see this in Psalm 100:3 where it says:

> **Know ye that the Lord he is God: it is he that hath made us, and not we ourselves....**

This means the universe didn't come into being by random chance, but by the creative command of God. He opened His mouth, and everything came into existence by His spoken word. Although we are living in a day when many people try to rule God out of creation, this is not an option for us as believers. The first affirmation of The Apostles' Creed points us to the true and living God who is our Father, who is Almighty, and who has created — and continues to sustain — everything that exists.

What does the Bible say about those who say God doesn't exist? Psalm 14:1 answers by saying, "The fool hath said in his heart, there is no God...."

Friend, The Apostles' Creed holds the nonnegotiable doctrines of the Christian faith for every church and for every Christian. Regarding these key foundational truths of the Christian faith, there is simply no room for negotiation. These are the immutable doctrines of our faith — and as such, they need to be taught, embraced, and affirmed.

In this late hour of the last days, it is vital that spiritual leaders acknowledge what they believe and accept the responsibility to speak accurately and clearly for God as His spokesmen and call the Church back to the authoritative voice of the Bible. We must dig our heels into Scripture and resolve to *receive* nothing, *believe* nothing, and *follow* nothing that cannot be found in or proved by the Bible.

STUDY QUESTIONS

> Study to shew thyself approved unto God, a workman that needeth not to be ashamed, rightly dividing the word of truth.
> — 2 Timothy 2:15

1. What do these passages of Scripture instruct you to do to help guard yourself and your loved ones from becoming one of the ones who "depart from the faith"?

    - 2 Timothy 3:15-17
    - John 8:31,32
    - Proverbs 4:20-22
    - John 15:4-8

2. The first statement of faith in The Apostles' Creed is that there is only one God, and it is in this One true God alone that we put our faith. Do you believe this? If not, why? What ideas cause you to question and doubt this foundational truth? Pray and ask the Holy Spirit to really solidify this truth in your heart and mind. (Consider Deuteronomy 6:4 and Jesus' words in Mark 12:29.)

3. The third declaration in The Apostles' Creed is the belief that God is the Creator of Heaven and earth. Why do you think this truth is so disputed in the world and even among some Christians? If you find yourself struggling to fully embrace this statement of faith, take some time to really chew on the truth in these passages from God's Word: Genesis 1:1; Nehemiah 9:6,7; Isaiah 42:5; John 1:3; Acts 17:24; Colossians 1:16,17; Revelation 4:11 and 10:5,6.

PRACTICAL APPLICATION

> But be ye doers of the word, and not hearers only, deceiving your own selves.
> — James 1:22

1. Take a few moments to carefully read through The Apostles' Creed. Are there any core beliefs that you see that you didn't realize were a foundational part of the Christian faith? If so, which one or ones?

2. Be honest. How would you describe your grasp on the basic, foundational truths of the Christian faith?

3. Through Paul, the Holy Spirit warns us that at the very end of the age, some believers will gradually withdraw and transition away from the Christian faith they once stood by and believed. In what ways are you seeing this happen in the world as well as in your immediate circle of relationships?

---

[1] Robin Ngo, "The Nicea Church: Where Did the Council of Nicea Meet?" Biblical Archaeology Society: Bible History Daily, April 9, 2021, https://www.biblicalarchaeology.org/daily/biblical-sites-places/biblical-archaeology-sites/nicea-church-council-of-nicea/

LESSON 2

TOPIC
Jesus Christ, His Only Son

SCRIPTURES
1. **1 Peter 3:18** — For Christ also hath once suffered for sins, the just for the unjust, that he might bring us to God, being put to death in the flesh, but quickened by the Spirit.
2. **Colossians 2:15** — And having spoiled principalities and powers, he made a shew of them openly, triumphing over them in it.
3. **Acts 2:36** — …God hath made the same Jesus, whom ye have crucified, both Lord and Christ.
4. **Colossians 1:18** — And he is the head of the body, the church: who is the beginning, the firstborn from the dead; that in all things he might have the preeminence.
5. **Philippians 2:9-11** — Wherefore God also hath highly exalted him, and given him a name which is above every name: that at the name of Jesus every knee should bow, of things in heaven, and things in earth, and things under the earth; and that every tongue should confess that Jesus Christ is Lord, to the glory of God the Father.
6. **Romans 10:9-13** — That if thou shalt confess with thy mouth the Lord Jesus, and shalt believe in thine heart that God hath raised him from the dead, thou shalt be saved. For with the heart man believeth unto righteousness; and with the mouth confession is made unto

salvation. For the scripture saith, Whosoever believeth on him shall not be ashamed. For there is no difference between the Jew and the Greek: for the same Lord over all is rich unto all that call upon him. For whosoever shall call upon the name of the Lord shall be saved.

GREEK WORDS

1. "spoiled" — ἀπεκδύομαι (*apekduomai*): to completely strip bare, as in ripping a garment or weapon off someone
2. "principalities" — τὰς ἀρχὰς (*tas archas*): the chief princes, the ruling principalities; referring to dark spiritual powers
3. "powers" — τὰς ἐξουσίας (*tas exousias*): influencing powers
4. "shew" — δειγματίζω (*deigmatidzo*): to expose, to make an example of, or to make a public example
5. "openly" — ἐν παρρησίᾳ (*en parresia*): in great boldness, with great frankness; indisputably
6. "triumphing" — θριαμβεύω (*thriambeuo*): to humiliatingly lead a prisoner or prisoners in a victorious triumphal parade
7. "Lord" — κύριος (*kurios*): lord or supreme master

SYNOPSIS

As we noted in Lesson 1, The Apostle's Creed dates back to approximately 140 AD in its oldest form and was earlier known as The Old Roman Creed. The Old Roman Creed is the earliest known creed of the Christian faith, and it's widely believed to be the first creed. In the late Fourth Century, an Early Church leader named Tyrannius Rufinus wrote a commentary on the creed where he recounted the viewpoint that the apostles originally authored together after Pentecost and before they left Jerusalem to preach elsewhere.

It seems that The Old Roman Creed is the very earliest statement of what was believed by the apostles. The Apostles' Creed is a revision, which was written in the year 390 AD, and the Early Church fathers referred to it as "the rule of faith." It is considered a condensed compilation of the teachings of the apostles, and thus the reason it is referred to as The Apostles' Creed.

The emphasis of this lesson:

Jesus is the eternal Son of God who was conceived of the Holy Spirit and born of the Virgin Mary. Through His death, burial, and resurrection He totally disarmed all the evil powers that were arrayed against us, parading them in humiliation before all the hosts of Heaven. Because Jesus humbled Himself so low, God has exalted Him as Lord and Christ over all.

The Apostles' Creed Contains the Foundational Beliefs of Our Faith

In The Apostles' Creed, we discover the unchallengeable core beliefs of the Christian faith, and through the centuries that followed, it was used as a "truth filter" to determine what was and wasn't genuine Christian doctrine. Today, The Apostles' Creed is still widely used in many denominational churches all over the world. Whole congregations, such as the Good News Church in Moscow, quote the creed regularly with confidence and joy, and it helps establish people in the truth of what we believe as Christians. Here is The Apostles' Creed:

> **I believe in God, the Father Almighty,**
> **the Creator of heaven and earth,**
> **and in Jesus Christ, His only Son, our Lord:**
> **Who was conceived of the Holy Spirit,**
> **born of the Virgin Mary,**
> **suffered under Pontius Pilate,**
> **was crucified, died, and was buried.**
> **He descended into hell.**
> **The third day He arose again from the dead.**
> **He ascended into heaven**
> **and sits at the right hand of God the Father Almighty,**
> **whence He shall come to judge the living and the dead.**
> **I believe in the Holy Spirit,**
> **the holy catholic [universal] church,**
> **the communion of saints,**

the forgiveness of sins,

the resurrection of the body,

and life everlasting. Amen.

'I Believe… in Jesus Christ, His Only Son, Our Lord'

The next major declaration of faith in The Apostles' Creed is that Jesus Christ is God's only Son, our Lord. Early Christians recognized that Jesus was God in their midst. That is the meaning of the word "Emmanuel" — God with us. Jesus is the eternal Son of God who was conceived of the Holy Spirit and born of the Virgin Mary. In His death on the Cross, He made provision for the redemption of men from sin, and on the third day, He was physically raised from the dead. Forty days later, He ascended into Heaven where He is seated at the Father's right hand as the Head of the Church.

Three Specific Accomplishments Through Jesus' Death

In First Peter 3:18, the apostle Peter wrote and said, "For Christ also hath once suffered for sins, the just for the unjust, that he might bring us to God, being put to death in the flesh, but quickened by the Spirit."

In this passage, we see three specific things Jesus accomplished through His death on the Cross. First, He died for our sins so that He could purchase our forgiveness. Second, He died as the righteous One in place of the unrighteous, which is us. Jesus took the penalty for all our wrongdoing and paid the wages for our sins with His death.

The third accomplishment Jesus made on the Cross was the restoration of our relationship with the Father. He died to bring us back to God. Without His death, we could not have a relationship with God.

The Apostles' Creed emphatically states that after Jesus' death, He was buried. It also says He descended into hell, which is a truth that some people struggle to believe. Yet, here we see it in The Apostles' Creed, which means the apostles believed it.

After Jesus' death, burial, and descent into hell, His resurrection took place on the third day. Once He returned to the Father, He was seated in a place of honor and authority at the Father's right hand, and He is coming again to bring judgment at the end of time. All five of these truths are enshrined in The Apostles' Creed, and we will carefully unpack each one in the coming lessons.

Through Jesus' Death and Resurrection He Soundly Defeated All Our Enemies

One of the most important results of Jesus' death on the Cross is found in Paul's letter to the church of Colossae. He declared, "And having spoiled principalities and powers, he [Jesus] made a shew of them openly, triumphing over them in it" (Colossians 2:15). There are six important words in this verse that you need to understand in order to more fully appreciate what Jesus did through His death.

The first word is "spoiled," which is the Greek word *apekduomai*, and it means *to completely strip bare, as in ripping a garment or weapon off someone*. Who did Jesus strip of clothing and weaponry? The Bible says "principalities," which is a translation of the Greek words *tas archas*. This describes *the chief princes, the ruling principalities*, and it refers back to *dark spiritual powers*. Before Jesus' sacrifice on the Cross, *principalities* ruled the world, but Jesus stripped these ancient evil forces of their power through His death, burial, and resurrection.

The Bible says He also stripped bare "powers." This word is a translation of the Greek words *tas exousias* and describes *influencing spiritual powers*. Jesus "...made a shew of them [principalities and powers] openly, triumphing over them in it" (Colossians 2:15). The word "shew" here is the Greek word *deigmatidzo*, which means *to expose, to make an example*, or *to make a public example with the purpose of humiliation*.

This brings us to the word "openly," which in Greek is *en parresia*, meaning *in great boldness, with great frankness*, or *indisputably*. The use of this word tells us that when Jesus stripped principalities and powers of their power, He did it with great boldness and frankness, and what He accomplished was indisputable.

Moreover, Colossians 2:15 says Jesus was "triumphing over them in it," and the word "triumphing" is the Greek word *thriambeuo*, which means *to humiliatingly lead a prisoner or prisoners in a victorious triumphal parade*. A great example of the word "triumphing" is seen in what happened when a great general would return to Rome after he conquered an enemy.

When he came into the city of Rome, he led a triumphal parade, and in a triumphal parade, the general rode in his chariot at the very front of the procession. Behind him were all the weapons of the enemy that he had seized — along with the foreign enemy now incarcerated in chains.

That enemy was made to humiliatingly walk behind the general who defeated him. All the city of Rome filled the streets to rejoice with the returning victor and to see the enemy who was paraded before them in chains and in absolute defeat. That is where this word *triumphing* comes from.

When we incorporate the original meaning of all these Greek words in Colossians 2:15, it tells us that after Jesus died on the Cross and was buried, He spent three days in hell, and while He was in hell, He utterly destroyed the enemy, stripping him of all his power and weapons. In His resurrection, Jesus returned like a great general returning victoriously after a battle. Behind Him, Satan and his demonic forces were displayed in humiliation with all their weapons now in Christ's custody. All of that happened in the death, burial, and resurrection of Jesus Christ. This was a significant part of Jesus' work when He came to earth as God's only Son.

Jesus Is Exalted as Lord and Christ!

Because Jesus so humbled himself, the Father has elevated Him high above all others. Peter confirmed this on the Day of Pentecost when he stood up and said, "…God hath made the same Jesus, whom ye have crucified, both *Lord* and *Christ*" (Acts 2:36). The word for "Lord" in this verse is the Greek word *kurios*, which means *lord* or *supreme master*.

The apostle Paul echoed this same truth in Colossians 1:18, which says, "And he is the head of the body, the church: who is the beginning, the firstborn from the dead; that in all things he might have the preeminence." Indeed, there is no one higher than the Lord Jesus Christ! Paul also speaks about this in his letter to the believers in Philippi saying:

> **Wherefore God also hath highly exalted him, and given him a name which is above every name: that at the name of Jesus every knee should bow, of things in heaven, and things in earth, and things under the earth; and that every tongue should confess that Jesus Christ is Lord, to the glory of God the Father.**
> **— Philippians 2:9-11**

The word "name" in this passage is the Greek word *onoma*, which could also be translated as *a reputation*. Jesus has a name or reputation that sparkles! It's unlike anyone else's. In fact, it is *above every other name!* And at the name of Jesus, every knee will bow, and every tongue will confess — in Heaven and in earth and under the earth — that Jesus Christ is Lord to the glory of God, the Father!

Once again, we see the word "Lord" — the Greek word *kurios*, meaning *the supreme master*, the One who is Lord over every realm — both visible and invisible. That is why these verses say that He is exalted above everything in Heaven, in the earth, and under the earth. He is preeminent above all in every realm.

Anyone Who Calls on the Name of the Lord Will Be Saved!

When we come to the book of Romans, the apostle Paul pens one of the most important passages in the Scriptures — one that tells us how we can be saved. Under the inspiration of the Holy Spirit, Paul wrote:

> **That if thou shalt confess with thy mouth the Lord Jesus, and shalt believe in thine heart that God hath raised him from the dead, thou shalt be saved.**
>
> **For with the heart man believeth unto righteousness; and with the mouth confession is made unto salvation.**
>
> **For the scripture saith, Whosoever believeth on him shall not be ashamed.**
>
> **For there is no difference between the Jew and the Greek: for the same Lord over all is rich unto all that call upon him.**
>
> **For whosoever shall call upon the name of the Lord shall be saved.**
> — **Romans 10:9-13**

Three times in these five verses, the word "Lord" appears, and it is again the Greek word *kurios*, meaning *lord* or *supreme master*. Hence, Jesus is Lord over all in every realm — visible and invisible. To "confess with your mouth that Jesus is Lord" means you willfully choose to declare Him as Lord and totally surrender your life to His supreme authority and absolute control.

When Paul says, "For there is no difference between the Jew and the Greek" (Romans 10:12), he is letting us know that God's offer of salvation is for anyone, regardless of ethnicity or skin color. **Absolutely anyone who calls on the name of the Lord will be saved!**

Friend, do you believe in Jesus Christ, God's only Son, our Lord? The apostles did, and it is part of The Apostles' Creed. Are you seeing the importance of reaffirming this as a part of our faith?

In our next lesson, we will turn our attention to the next point in The Apostles' Creed: "[He] was conceived by the Holy Spirit, born of the Virgin Mary."

STUDY QUESTIONS

> Study to shew thyself approved unto God, a workman that needeth not to be ashamed, rightly dividing the word of truth.
> — 2 Timothy 2:15

1. Take some time to reflect upon the original Greek meaning of Colossians 2:15 and in your own words describe what it says Christ did for *you* through the work of the Cross. How does this truth encourage you and breathe new life into your faith?
2. Through Jesus' death, burial, and resurrection He defeated the enemy and positioned us in victory. Look up these verses and write out what God has promised you through the finished work of Jesus, His Son.
   - Luke 10:19
   - Matthew 16:19 and 18:18-20
   - Romans 8:35-39
   - 2 Corinthians 2:14

PRACTICAL APPLICATION

> But be ye doers of the word, and not hearers only, deceiving your own selves.
> — James 1:22

1. Interestingly, Joel 2:32, Acts 2:21 and Romans 10:13 all declare the exact same promise: "Everyone who calls on the name of the Lord will be saved." In addition to the moment you called on Jesus and

received God's saving grace, can you think of another time when you called out the name "Jesus" and His saving power showed up? What happened? How did calling out to Jesus rescue you from trouble?
2. Throughout the New Testament, Jesus is called "Lord," which is the Greek word *Kurios*, meaning *lord* or *supreme master*. This means He is the one who calls the shots in our life, and what He says is what we're to do. Be honest: Does Jesus hold the position of "Lord" in your life? In what areas do you find it difficult to submit to His lordship?
3. Take a moment to pray: *Lord, please forgive me for not fully obeying You* (name anything specific that comes to mind). *Please give me the grace to truly trust You in every area of my life. In Jesus' name. Amen.*

LESSON 3

TOPIC
Born of the Virgin Mary

SCRIPTURES
1. **Luke 2:19** — But Mary kept all these things, and pondered them in her heart.
2. **Isaiah 11:1** — And there shall come forth a rod out of the stem of Jesse, and a Branch shall grow out of his roots.
3. **Luke 2:4** — And Joseph also went up from Galilee, out of the city of Nazareth, into Judaea, unto the city of David, which is called Bethlehem; (because he was of the house and lineage of David).
4. **Luke 1:32** — He shall be great, and shall be called the Son of the Highest: and the Lord God shall give unto him the throne of his father David.
5. **Luke 1:69** — [God] hath raised up an horn of salvation for us in the house of his servant David.
6. **Romans 1:3** — Concerning his Son Jesus Christ our Lord, which was made of the seed of David according to the flesh.
7. **Luke 1:26,27** — And in the sixth month the angel Gabriel was sent from God unto a city of Galilee, named Nazareth, to a virgin

espoused to a man whose name was Joseph, of the house of David; and the virgin's name was Mary.

8. **Isaiah 7:14** — Therefore the Lord himself shall give you a sign; behold, a virgin shall conceive, and bear a son, and shall call his name Immanuel.

9. **Luke 1:28,29** — And the angel came in unto her, and said, Hail, thou that art highly favoured, the Lord is with thee: blessed art thou among women. And when she saw him, she was troubled at his saying, and cast in her mind what manner of salutation this should be.

10. **Luke 1:31-35,38** — And, behold, thou shalt conceive in thy womb, and bring forth a son, and shalt call his name Jesus. He shall be great, and shall be called the Son of the Highest: and the Lord God shall give unto him the throne of his father David: And he shall reign over the house of Jacob for ever; and of his kingdom there shall be no end. Then said Mary unto the angel, How shall this be, seeing I know not a man? And the angel answered and said unto her, The Holy Ghost shall come upon thee, and the power of the Highest shall overshadow thee: therefore also that holy thing which shall be born of thee shall be called the Son of God.... And Mary said, Behold the handmaid of the Lord; be it unto me according to thy word. And the angel departed from her.

11. **Matthew 1:18** — Now the birth of Jesus Christ was on this wise: When as his mother Mary was espoused to Joseph, before they came together, she was found with child of the Holy Ghost.

12. **Luke 2:7** — And she brought forth her firstborn son, and wrapped him in swaddling clothes, and laid him in a manger....

GREEK WORDS

1. "kept" — συντηρέω (*suntereo*): to keep within oneself in order to closely guard or to accurately and carefully preserve
2. "ponder" — συμβάλλω (*sumballo*): to lay in order, like one who carefully and meticulously chronicles a story
3. "Nazareth" — (Hebrew, *netzer*): a word that means a shoot or a branch

SYNOPSIS

So far, we've seen that The Apostles' Creed dates back to approximately 140 AD in its oldest form and was originally known as The Old Roman Creed. But its present form likely dates to approximately 390 AD. It is called The Apostles' Creed because it is a condensed compilation of the teachings of the apostles. Early Church fathers referred to it as "the rule of faith," and it covers the unchallengeable core beliefs of the Christian faith.

In the centuries that followed, The Apostles' Creed was used like a "truth filter" to determine what was and wasn't genuine Christian doctrine. Even today, The Apostles' Creed is still widely used in churches all over the world, and each week entire congregations confidently quote the creed, reaffirming the fundamentals of the Christian faith in which they believe.

Multitudes have found that quoting The Apostles' Creed is very helpful in reminding them of what they believe. If you think about it, there are many people in churches today from agnostic, atheistic, and pagan backgrounds. By quoting The Apostles' Creed, we very succinctly state what we as Christians believe, and that audible confession strengthens and deepens our understanding of the faith.

The emphasis of this lesson:

Jesus is the Son of God, not the biological son of Joseph His earthly father. Mary, who had no sexual relations with any man, became pregnant when the Holy Spirit of God came upon her. Jesus — the firstborn Son that was born to her — was fathered by God Himself.

A Brief Review of Lessons 1 and 2

In our first lesson, we examined the opening words of The Apostles' Creed, which state, "I believe in God, the Father Almighty, the Creator of heaven and earth." We saw how this statement, declaring faith in the One True God, may seem simple, but it's vital in our age when many are doubting the very existence of God. And even if they do believe He exists, some question whether He really created Heaven and earth. The Apostles' Creed affirms the One True God who is our Father and Creator of all things.

The creed goes on to say, "I believe… in Jesus Christ, His only Son, our Lord." In our last lesson, we saw what Jesus accomplished on the Cross for us and how He soundly defeated all the powers of darkness. And because

Jesus humbled Himself to die in our place, God elevated Him to be our Lord, which means He is Supreme Master over everything and everyone in every realm. Every time we say *Jesus is Lord*, we are surrendering control of our lives completely to His will.

Here again is The Apostles' Creed:

> **I believe in God, the Father Almighty,**
> **the Creator of heaven and earth,**
> **and in Jesus Christ, His only Son, our Lord:**
> **Who was conceived of the Holy Spirit,**
> **born of the Virgin Mary,**
> **suffered under Pontius Pilate,**
> **was crucified, died, and was buried.**
> **He descended into hell.**
> **The third day He arose again from the dead.**
> **He ascended into heaven**
> **and sits at the right hand of God the Father Almighty,**
> **whence He shall come to judge the living and the dead.**
> **I believe in the Holy Spirit,**
> **the holy catholic [universal] church,**
> **the communion of saints,**
> **the forgiveness of sins,**
> **the resurrection of the body,**
> **and life everlasting. Amen.**

'I Believe… [Jesus] Was Conceived by the Holy Spirit, Born of the Virgin Mary'

The next nonnegotiable truth in *The Apostle's Creed* centers on the truth of Jesus' virgin birth, which is very important because it is a declaration that Jesus is the Son of God, not the son of Joseph.

Mary kept records of Jesus' birth. The bulk of what we know about the events surrounding His nativity comes directly from Mary herself. Before

Luke wrote in his gospel about the birth of Jesus, he first interviewed Mary while she lived in Ephesus where she had moved with the apostle John later in her life. It was Mary herself who vividly told Luke about all the miraculous events that he wrote about in his gospel. Mary's memory of these astounding events is referred to in Luke 2:19, where the Bible says:

> **But Mary kept all these things, and pondered them in her heart.**

Note the word "kept" in this verse. It is the Greek word *suntereo*, and it means *to keep within oneself in order to closely guard or to accurately and carefully preserve*. And the Greek word for "ponder" here is *sumballo*, which means *to lay in order, like one who carefully and meticulously chronicles a story*. Mary was so impacted by this amazing sequence of events in her life and in the life of Jesus that she chronicled all of it in her heart and carefully preserved her memories of it.

What we know about Nazareth: The Scriptures also tell us that the angel Gabriel came to Mary while she was living in Galilee — to a very obscure town called *Nazareth*. Although Nazareth is named in the New Testament, very little is known about it from ancient sources. It was such a small, agricultural village that archaeological research concludes that in Jesus' time, it is likely that no more than 200 people lived there. In fact, Nazareth was so "off the beaten track" that there was no reason for people to even go there unless they just wanted to visit someone.

Apparently, the little village of Nazareth was so inconsequential that in John 1:46, Nathanael asked the question, "Can anything good come out of Nazareth?" Still, we know that the word "Nazareth" — the Hebrew word *netzer* — describes *a shoot* or *a branch*. This helps us understand why Isaiah gave a Messianic prophecy that said, "And there shall come forth a rod out of the stem of Jesse, and a Branch shall grow out of his roots" (Isaiah 11:1).

The word "branch" in this verse is the Hebrew word *netzer* — the same word the name Nazareth comes from. Some scholars imply that the town of Nazareth was so called because it was the place where a "branch" of David lived, referring to a branch of David's family. Interestingly, in 100 BC one clan from the line of David did move there, so Nazareth did become home to one branch of David's line.

Joseph and Mary were descendants of David. Evidence points to the fact that the holy family — Joseph, Mary, and Jesus — were descendants of David, and that is why the angel Gabriel announced to Mary that Christ would sit upon the throne of His father David. Jesus was literally born into the royal Davidic line — part of whom lived in Nazareth. Luke 2:4 specifically states that *Joseph*, "…was of the house and lineage of David."

Again and again, the Bible speaks of Jesus' connection to David. In Luke 1:32, the angel Gabriel said, "…The Lord God shall give unto him the throne of *his father David*" (Luke 1:32). Similarly, Luke 1:69 says, "[God] hath raised up an horn of salvation for us *in the house of his servant David.*" The apostle Paul also wrote about Christ's connection with the lineage of David, saying, "Concerning [God's] Son Jesus Christ our Lord, which was made *of the seed of David* according to the flesh" (Romans 1:3). This is important for us to grasp because it means Mary carried royal blood in her veins.

One scholar has rightly noted that if Mary had not *herself* been a descendant of David, Jesus could not have been born "of the seed of David." This is also made clear in Luke 1:26 and 27, which says, "And in the sixth month the angel Gabriel was sent from God unto a city of Galilee, named Nazareth, to a virgin espoused to a man whose name was Joseph, *of the house of David*; and the virgin's name was Mary." The words "of the house of David" in Greek can refer to both Joseph and Mary who were each of royal descent.

Christ's Virgin-Birth Was a Supernatural Fulfillment of Prophecy

Notice in Luke 1:26 that Gabriel made his announcement "to a virgin." Mary being "a virgin" was a fulfillment of Isaiah 7:14, which says, "Therefore the Lord himself shall give you a sign; Behold, a virgin shall conceive, and bear a son, and shall call his name Immanuel." The fact that the word "Immanuel" means *God with us*, shoots down the skeptics' claim that the word "virgin" simply means Mary was *a young girl* or *a young maiden*.

The word translated "virgin" in the original Greek categorically means Mary was a real virgin who had never experienced a sexual relationship — not ever — with a man. When the angel Gabriel first appeared to Mary, he said, "…Hail, thou that art highly favoured, the Lord is with thee: blessed art thou among women" (Luke 1:28). The Bible goes on to say,

"And when she saw him, she was troubled at his saying, and cast in her mind what manner of salutation this should be" (Luke 1:29).

The phrase "cast in her mind" means this announcement pushed Mary to the limits of her understanding, and she was struggling to grasp the full meaning of what Gabriel was announcing to her. How could she be so "blessed among women" when she hadn't yet experienced a sexual relationship with a man? Gabriel then began to explain what was about to take place:

> **And, behold, thou shalt conceive in thy womb, and bring forth a son, and shalt call his name Jesus.**
>
> **He shall be great, and shall be called the Son of the Highest: and the Lord God shall give unto him the throne of his father David:**
>
> **And he shall reign over the house of Jacob for ever; and of his kingdom there shall be no end.**
>
> — Luke 1:31-33

The word "behold" in verse 31 is the Greek word *idou*, which denotes a sense of *amazement* or *bewilderment*. It is the interjection of Gabriel's own sentiment into the announcement that he was about to make to Mary. In essence, Gabriel was saying, *"Wow, what I'm about to tell you is so amazing it nearly leaves me speechless…."*

The angel then told Mary, "…Thou shalt conceive in thy womb…" (Luke 1:31). Notice this was a conception that occurred in the womb — without the participation of a man. Gabriel went on to tell her that she would give birth to a son and He would be called the Son of the Highest. Indeed, this would be a divine conception inside the womb of Mary without the participation of a man. God Himself would supernaturally cause Mary to be impregnated by the power of the Holy Spirit.

It's no wonder that Mary would respond by saying, "…How shall this be, seeing I know not a man? And the angel answered and said unto her, The Holy Ghost shall come upon thee, and the power of the Highest shall overshadow thee: therefore also that holy thing which shall be born of thee shall be called the Son of God" (Luke 1:34,35).

Gabriel made it clear to Mary that she would become impregnated supernaturally as the power of the Holy Spirit came upon her. When Mary understood, she simply surrendered and said, "…Behold the handmaid of the Lord; be it unto me according to thy word. And the angel departed from her" (Luke 1:38).

Mary Became Pregnant With Jesus While She Was 'Espoused' to Joseph

It's important to note that the Bible specifically states that when "…Mary was espoused to Joseph, *before they came together*, she was found with child of the Holy Ghost" (Matthew 1:18). In other words, before Mary came together sexually with Joseph, she was found to be pregnant with Jesus. In biblical times, Jewish girls were eligible to be "espoused" at the age of *12 years and 6 months*. Most scholars believe that Mary was somewhere between the ages of 12 and 14 when she became "espoused" to Joseph.

What does it mean to be "espoused"? In one sense, it depicts an *engagement*, but unlike modern engagements that can be broken, an "espousal" among the Jews was a legally binding agreement. Even though the future spouses did not live together and had no sexual relationship during the espousal period, if one's espousal was to be terminated, it could only be broken legally by divorce. So, when young Jewish men and women entered into the espousal period, they did so very seriously, because it was a lifelong commitment that could only be broken in a Jewish court of law.

Among Jews, marriage was started with an espousal period that was initiated with a public announcement. Once that announcement was made, the bride and groom legally belonged to each other — though they did not live together until about a year later when the marriage was to be publicly celebrated and then sexually consummated.

It was during this time of preparation and waiting — before they came together — that Mary "…was found with child of the Holy Ghost" (Matthew 1:18). At the full, appointed time, the Bible says, "And she brought forth her firstborn son, and wrapped him in swaddling clothes, and laid him in a manger…" (Luke 2:7).

Friend, Jesus was born supernaturally! Mary became pregnant by the power of the Holy Spirit before she knew any man sexually. Jesus' birth was a virgin birth, and this is a vital part of our faith. He was not the offspring of a man, but the Son of God! In our next lesson, we'll see that The Apostles' Creed goes on to say that Jesus suffered under Pontius Pilate.

STUDY QUESTIONS

> Study to shew thyself approved unto God, a workman that
> needeth not to be ashamed, rightly dividing the word of truth.
> — 2 Timothy 2:15

1. What new facts did you learn about the city of Nazareth? And what new facts did you learn about Joseph and Mary's connection to David?
2. Why do you think it's significant that both Joseph *and* Mary were descendants of David?
3. Just as the Holy Spirit came upon Mary and she conceived God's Son, when someone gets saved, the Holy Spirit comes upon that person and deposits the spiritual Seed of God into them. It is what Jesus described to Nicodemus as being *born again* in John 3:3-8. Take a few moments to read this passage along with John 1:12,13; First John 3:9; and First Peter 1:23. What is the Holy Spirit showing you about your spiritual birth into the family of God?

PRACTICAL APPLICATION

> But be ye doers of the word, and not hearers only,
> deceiving your own selves.
> — James 1:22

1. This lesson focuses on the statement of faith that Jesus *was conceived of the Holy Spirit, born of the Virgin Mary*. Clearly, this is what the Bible says and what the apostles believed. But do *you* believe it? Why do you think it was so crucial that Jesus be fathered by God Himself and not just a good man of earth?
2. Under the inspiration of the Holy Spirit, Paul wrote Romans 5:12-21, comparing Adam who disobeyed God in the Garden of Eden with Jesus, who obeyed God even to the point of death. As you read through these verses, identify what Adam lost for himself and humanity and what Jesus recovered that no one else could. (Also consider First Corinthians 15:21,22.)
3. What is the Holy Spirit showing you in Romans 5:12-21 that Jesus personally provided for you?

LESSON 4

TOPIC
Suffered Under Pontius Pilate

SCRIPTURES

1. **Luke 23:2** — And they began to accuse him, saying, We found this fellow perverting the nation, and forbidding to give tribute to Caesar, saying that he himself is Christ a King.
2. **Matthew 27:2** — And when they had bound him, they led him away, and delivered him to Pontius Pilate the governor.
3. **Matthew 27:11-14** — And Jesus stood before the governor: and the governor asked him, saying, Art thou the King of the Jews? And Jesus said unto him, Thou sayest. And when he was accused of the chief priests and elders, he answered nothing. Then said Pilate unto him, Hearest thou not how many things they witness against thee? And he answered him to never a word; insomuch that the governor marvelled greatly.
4. **Luke 23:3,4** — And Pilate asked him, saying, Art thou the King of the Jews? And he answered him and said, Thou sayest it. Then said Pilate to the chief priests and to the people, I find no fault in this man.
5. **John 19:12** — And from thenceforth Pilate sought to release him [Jesus]....
6. **Luke 23:14-16** — ...Ye have brought this man unto me, as one that perverteth the people: and, behold, I, having examined him before you, have found no fault in this man touching those things whereof ye accuse him: no, nor yet Herod: for I sent you to him; and, lo, nothing worthy of death is done unto him. I will therefore chastise him, and release him.
7. **Luke 23:20-23** — Pilate therefore, willing to release Jesus, spake again to them. But they cried, saying, Crucify him, crucify him. And he said unto them a third time, Why, what evil hath he done? I have found no cause of death in him: I will therefore chastise him, and let him go. And they were instant with loud voices, requiring that he might be crucified....

8. **Matthew 27:24** — When Pilate saw that he could prevail nothing, but that rather a tumult was made, he took water, and washed his hands before the multitude, saying, I am innocent of the blood of this just person: see ye to it.
9. **Matthew 27:26** — …And when he had scourged Jesus, he delivered him to be crucified.
10. **Isaiah 53:5** — But he was wounded for our transgressions, he was bruised for our iniquities: the chastisement of our peace was upon him; and with his stripes we are healed.
11. **1 Timothy 6:13** — I give thee charge in the sight of God, who quickeneth all things, and before Christ Jesus, who before Pontius Pilate witnessed a good confession.

GREEK WORDS

1. "bound" — δήσαντες (*desantes*): from the word δέω (*deo*), the same word that was used to describe the binding, tying up, or securing of an animal
2. "led him away" — ἀπάγω (*apago*): used for a shepherd who tied a rope around the neck of his sheep and then led it down the path where it needed to go
3. "delivered" — παραδίδωμι (*paradidomi*): to commit, to deliver, or to hand something over to someone else
4. "marveled greatly" — θαυμάζω (*thaumadzo*): to wonder, to be at a loss of words, or to be shocked and amazed
5. "examined" — ἀνακρίνας (*anakrinas*): to examine closely, to scrutinize, or to judge judicially
6. "cried" — ἐπιφωνέω (*epiphoneo*): to shout, to scream, to yell, to shriek, or to screech; the tense means they were hysterically screaming and shrieking at the top of their voices — totally out of control and without pause

SYNOPSIS

We've seen that what is called The Apostles' Creed dates back to approximately 140 AD in its oldest form and was earlier known as the Old Roman Creed. Its present form, which is the one we use today, likely dates to approximately 390 AD. Early Church fathers referred to it as "the rule of faith." It is a condensed compilation of the teachings of the apostles, and thus the reason it is referred to as The Apostles' Creed.

This historic creed covers the unchallengeable, core beliefs of the Christian faith, and in the centuries that followed, it was used by the Early Church as a "truth filter" to determine what was and wasn't genuine Christian doctrine. Today, The Apostles' Creed is still widely used in denominations all over the world.

The truth is we are living in a day when all kinds of erroneous teachings are being disseminated in churches and on the Internet. Being mindful of what the apostles believed and taught is vital to knowing the basic beliefs of the Christian faith and therefore being able to recognize what is and what is not sound teaching.

The emphasis of this lesson:

Pontius Pilate was a real person who ruled as governor of Judea the entire time of Jesus' ministry. Although he had a staunch reputation for being brutal, he knew Jesus was innocent and wanted to release Him. But when the political pressure became intense, he gave into the demands of the Jewish leaders and had Jesus scourged and then crucified.

A Review of The Apostles' Creed

The Church has been and continues to be made up of people from diverse backgrounds, including some that are educated and some uneducated; some with theological learning and others who are unbelieving pagans or even atheists. By knowing and reciting The Apostles' Creed, we all come together on the same page and begin to understand what we believe. Here again is The Apostles' Creed:

I believe in God, the Father Almighty,
the Creator of heaven and earth,
and in Jesus Christ, His only Son, our Lord:
Who was conceived of the Holy Spirit,
born of the Virgin Mary,
suffered under Pontius Pilate,
was crucified, died, and was buried.

He descended into hell.

The third day He arose again from the dead.

He ascended into heaven

and sits at the right hand of God the Father Almighty,

whence He shall come to judge the living and the dead.

I believe in the Holy Spirit,

the holy catholic [universal] church,

the communion of saints,

the forgiveness of sins,

the resurrection of the body,

and life everlasting. Amen.

'I Believe… [Jesus] Suffered Under Pontius Pilate'

The fourth major, nonnegotiable doctrine the apostles agreed upon is the declaration of faith that Jesus *"suffered under Pontius Pilate."* When The Apostles' Creed was compiled, which was approximately 140 AD, they had access to the legal records confirming that Jesus did indeed suffer under Pilate. So, rather than just being hearsay, this is a matter of historical documentation.

What Does History Tell Us About Pontius Pilate and Roman Rule?

At the time of Jesus' earthly ministry, Israel was overwhelmed with paranoid leaders who were obsessed with holding on to power. The political leaders installed by Rome over Israel were looking into every nook and cranny for opponents as they were constantly struggling to maintain their control of the region.

Now Israel despised the Romans for several reasons. First and foremost were their pagan tendencies. The Jews also couldn't stand the Romans constantly pushing their language and culture on them, and the taxes they were required to pay to Rome were simply infuriating.

What's interesting is that because of the political turmoil in Israel, few political leaders held power for very long, and those who did maintain their position did it by using cruelty and brutality. Thus, the ability to rule for a long duration required a ruthless leader who was willing to do anything necessary to maintain power.

This leads us to Pontius Pilate who was just that type of leader. The Jewish historian Flavius Josephus wrote that Pilate was ruthless, unsympathetic, and indifferent to how important the Jews' religious beliefs and convictions were to them. Normally, a governor in this region would serve for 12 to 36 months. But Pilate ruled as the governor of Judea for *ten* years — from 26 AD to 36 AD. It was during this specific span of time that Jesus' entire public ministry took place.

In addition to the normal responsibilities a governor possessed, Pilate was also the supreme authority in legal matters in the land. As the highest expert in Roman law, he had the final say-so in nearly all legal decisions for the territory of Judea. The only time he handed off a case was when it had to do with religious matters, which he dreaded. So Pilate sent these cases to the Sanhedrin to deal with.

Although Pilate did not actually live in Jerusalem, he would come to the city at the time of the Jewish feasts when it was filled with guests, travelers, and strangers. Because there was a greater potential for disorder and chaos during those times, Pilate and his troops would make their presence visibly known to maintain and protect the peace. Hence, that is why Pilate was in the city of Jerusalem at the time of Jesus' crucifixion.

Politics Played a Part in Pilate's Decision

The day the Jewish high priest, the Sanhedrin, and the huge mob that accompanied them demanded that Jesus be crucified, Pilate asked them the reason for their demand. They answered, "…We found this fellow perverting the nation, and forbidding to give tribute to Caesar, saying that he himself is Christ a King" (Luke 23:2).

Pilate knew the Jews were jealous of Jesus, but the charges they brought against Him put Pilate in a bad position politically. Clearly, he was a political man and knew how to play the political game. But what if the news reached Rome — that Jesus was perverting the nation, teaching people to withhold their taxes, and that He claimed to be a counter King in place of the Roman emperor? It would be political suicide for Pilate to do nothing.

The Jewish leaders were well aware of this when they fabricated their charges against Jesus. They knew exactly what political strings to pull to get Pilate to do what they wanted — and they were pulling every string they held in their hands.

Jesus Was Treated Like an Animal

The Bible says, "And when they had bound him [Jesus], they led him away, and delivered him to Pontius Pilate the governor" (Matthew 27:2). The word "bound" here is the Greek word *desantes*, which is from the word *deo*, the same word used to describe *the binding, tying up*, or *securing of an animal*.

Once Jesus was bound, the officers "led him away." This phrase is a translation of the Greek word *apago*, which was used to depict *a shepherd who tied a rope around the neck of his sheep and then led it down the path where it needed to go*. Just imagine: a rope was secured around the neck of King Jesus, and He was walked as the Lamb of God to Pontius Pilate. This confirms what Isaiah had prophesied nearly 700 years before Christ came — that He would be like a "lamb led to the slaughter" (*see* Isaiah 53:7).

Matthew then tells us the religious leaders "…delivered him to Pontius Pilate the governor" (Matthew 27:2). The word "delivered" is a form of the Greek word *paradidomi*, which means *to commit, to deliver*, or *to hand something over to someone else*. This tells us that when the high priest ordered Jesus to be taken to Pilate, he made Jesus Pilate's problem. The high priest delivered Him fully into Pilate's hands and then left Pilate with the responsibility to find Jesus guilty and to crucify Him.

The 'Three Strikes and You're Guilty' Rule

The Scripture then says, "And Jesus stood before the governor: and the governor asked him, saying, Art thou the King of the Jews? And Jesus said unto him, Thou sayest" (Matthew 27:11). Please note that this was the first time Jesus had been given the opportunity to defend Himself, and He refused to directly answer Pilate's question.

Matthew goes on to tell us, "And when he [Jesus] was accused of the chief priests and elders, he answered nothing" (Matthew 27:12). Here we see for a second time Jesus had a chance to refute the charges that were brought against Him, but again He refused to answer. "Then said Pilate unto him, Hearest thou not how many things they witness against thee? And he answered him to never a word; insomuch that the governor marvelled greatly" (Matthew 27:13,14).

The words "marveled greatly" are a translation of the Greek word *thaumadzo*, which means *to wonder*, *to be at a loss of words*, or *to be shocked and amazed*. Pilate was dumbfounded by Jesus' silence because Roman law gave prisoners three chances to defend themselves. If a prisoner passed up those three chances and refused to speak in his own defense, he would automatically be charged as "guilty."

Jesus passed up His *first chance* to defend Himself in Matthew 27:11 and His *second chance* in verse 12. Matthew 27:14 records the third opportunity Jesus had to defend Himself, which He also turned down. So according to Roman law, Jesus should have automatically been charged as guilty, but Pilate didn't want to crucify Him.

After hearing Jesus' responses, "Then said Pilate to the chief priests and to the people, I find no fault in this man" (Luke 23:4). The apostle John tells us, "And from thenceforth Pilate sought to release him…" (John 19:12).

Pilate Had Judicially 'Examined' Jesus

At this point, Pilate spoke to the Jewish leaders and said, "…Ye have brought this man unto me, as one that perverteth the people: and, behold, I, having examined him before you, have found no fault in this man touching those things whereof ye accuse him: no, nor yet Herod: for I sent you to him; and, lo, nothing worthy of death is done unto him. I will therefore chastise him, and release him" (Luke 23:14-16).

Notice Pilate said he "examined" Jesus. This word is a form of the Greek word *anakrinas*, which is a compound of the word *ana* and a form of the word *krino*. The word *ana* means *to do something again and again*, and the word *krino* means *to judicially examine* or *to judicially judge*. When these words are compounded to form *anakrinas*, it means Pilate had *examined*, *scrutinized*, and *closely judged Jesus judicially*, and he couldn't find a single crime that Jesus had committed. Thus, from a purely legal standpoint, Jesus was innocent.

Keep in mind, Pilate was the highest legal authority in the land. "Pilate therefore, willing to release Jesus, spake again to them. But they cried, saying, Crucify him, crucify him" (Luke 23:20,21). The word "cried" here is taken from the Greek word *epiphoneo*, and it means *to shout*, *to scream*, *to yell*, *to shriek*, or *to screech*. The tense of this word indicates that they were *hysterically screaming and shrieking at the top of their voices* — totally out of control and without pause.

Pilate again attempted to appeal to the Jewish leaders and the mob of people. "And he said unto them a third time, Why, what evil hath he done? I have found no cause of death in him: I will therefore chastise him, and let him go. And they were instant with loud voices, requiring that he might be crucified…" (Luke 23:22,23).

Matthew 27:24 continues the narrative saying, "When Pilate saw that he could prevail nothing, but that rather a tumult was made, he took water, and washed his hands before the multitude, saying, I am innocent of the blood of this just person: see ye to it." Historically, the washing of one's hands was a ritual often used to symbolically communicate, "I have no guilt in the matter."

Jesus Received the Roman 'Scourge'

As promised, Pilate chastised Jesus by having Him scourged. A "scourge" was one of the most horrific weapons in the ancient world. The mere threat of a scourging could calm a crowd or bend the will of the strongest rebel. According to Jewish law in Deuteronomy 25:3, Jews were permitted to give 40 lashes to a victim. However, because the fortieth lash often proved fatal, the Jewish authorities usually gave only 39 lashes.

In Jesus' case, it was the Romans who administered the scourging, and they had no limit to the number of lashes they could give a victim. It is likely they gave vast numbers of lashes to Him. As dreadful as the crucifixion was, it was only part of what Jesus endured. The scourging ripped His flesh to shreds, producing a full-body bruise. Indeed, as Isaiah 53:5 says, "…He was wounded for our transgressions, he was bruised for our iniquities: the chastisement of our peace was upon him; and with his stripes we are healed" (Isaiah 53:5). The lashes Christ received left stripes on His body, and it is those stripes that purchased our physical, mental, and emotional healing. Matthew 27:26 goes on to say, "…And when he had scourged Jesus, he delivered him to be crucified."

The apostle Paul tells us in First Timothy 6:13 that Jesus Christ "witnessed a good confession" before Pontius Pilate, which means Jesus never denied the truth of who He was — even in the face of death. This is the last mention of Pilate in the New Testament. Historical records show that some sort of accusations were brought against Pilate in the year 36 AD, and that charge resulted in his removal from office and exile to Gaul (modern-day France).

Eusebius — the well-known early Christian historian — later wrote that Pilate fell into misfortune under the wicked Emperor Caligula and lost many of his privileges. Eusebius also wrote that Pilate — who had ruled Judea ruthlessly and mercilessly for ten years and who was responsible for the trial, judgment, crucifixion, and burial of Jesus — finally committed suicide.

Friend, the statement in The Apostles' Creed about Jesus suffering before Pontius Pilate is legal proof that it really did occur. Jesus endured all the pain and suffering He went through for you and all of humanity.

STUDY QUESTIONS

Study to shew thyself approved unto God, a workman that needeth not to be ashamed, rightly dividing the word of truth.
— 2 Timothy 2:15

1. What did you learn about Pontius Pilate regarding his character, the way he interrogated Jesus, and how his life ended? How about the torture Jesus endured *before* even reaching the Cross?
2. Take some time to read Isaiah 53:1-7, which contains Isaiah's prophecies about Jesus' death. What stands out to you? What did His life, scourging, and death purchase for us?
3. Carefully reflect on the words of the psalmist in Psalm 22:1-8, reading it as if it were Jesus' thoughts on the Cross. What do you hear in His words that you've never heard before?

PRACTICAL APPLICATION

But be ye doers of the word, and not hearers only, deceiving your own selves.
— James 1:22

1. Does it change your perspective of Pontius Pilate to know what kind of a person he was and how long he'd been in power? How does it affect your mental picture of the story of Jesus' crucifixion to know

that even Pilate — one of the most brutal governors Judea had ever had — tried *on purpose* to get Jesus released?
2. Have you ever found yourself face to face with a "Pilate"? Someone who seemed to run over everyone in their path, willing to do whatever it took to stay at the top? How did you respond?
3. When reading Isaiah 53:5, which phrase hits you the hardest? What do *you* need healing from, whether physically, mentally, emotionally, or otherwise? Take a minute to tell Jesus where you're hurting, focusing on the price He paid for your restoration and inviting Him to make you well in all the places you've been broken.

LESSON 5

TOPIC
Crucified, Dead, and Buried

SCRIPTURES

1. **Matthew 27:31** — ...[They] led him away to crucify him.
2. **Matthew 27:33,35** — And when they were come unto a place called Golgotha, that is to say, a place of a skull... And they crucified him....
3. **John 19:28** — After this, Jesus knowing that all things were now accomplished, that the scripture might be fulfilled, saith, I thirst.
4. **John 19:30** — ...[Jesus] said, It is finished: and he bowed his head, and gave up the ghost.
5. **John 19:41,42** — Now in the place where he was crucified there was a garden; and in the garden a new sepulchre, wherein was never man yet laid. There laid they Jesus....
6. **Luke 23:55** — Beheld the sepulchre, and how his body was laid.
7. **Matthew 27:60** — ...and he [Joseph] rolled a great stone to the door of the sepulchre, and departed.
8. **Matthew 27:63-66** — Saying, Sir, we remember that that deceiver said, while he was yet alive, After three days I will rise again. Command therefore that the sepulchre be made sure until the third day, lest his disciples come by night, and steal him away, and say unto the people, He is risen from the dead: so the last error shall be worse than

the first. Pilate said unto them, Ye have a watch: go your way, make it as sure as ye can. So they went, and made the sepulchre sure, sealing the stone, and setting a watch.

9. **Acts 2:23,24** — …Ye have taken, and by wicked hands have crucified and slain [Jesus]: whom God hath raised up, having loosed the pains of death: because it was not possible that he should be holden of it.

SYNOPSIS

At a time when a great deal of false doctrine was being propagated in the Second Century Church, Early Church leaders assembled together and decided to document the most important beliefs of the Christian faith. The resulting document is called The Apostles' Creed. It succinctly states what we as Christians believe. Churches across the world still use The Apostles' Creed as a means to audibly declare in unity the nonnegotiable tenets of the Christian faith.

The emphasis of this lesson:

The death of Jesus Christ was not a hoax. History documents that He was tried by Pontius Pilate, scourged, and executed by crucifixion. Again and again, His death was verified by those who loved Him *and* those who hated Him. The Roman government confirmed Jesus' death and placed its seal on His tomb — and then posted soldiers to prevent anyone from tampering with His body.

A Quick Review of The Apostles' Creed and Its Origin

What is called The Apostle's Creed dates back to approximately 140 AD in its oldest form, which was earlier known as The Old Roman Creed. But its present form likely dates to approximately 390 AD. Early Church fathers referred to it as "the rule of faith," and it is a condensed compilation of the teachings of the apostles — thus, the reason it is referred to as The Apostles' Creed.

As we've noted, this creed documents the sacred and undisputable core beliefs of the Christian faith. In the centuries that followed, The Apostles' Creed was used like a "truth filter" to determine what was and wasn't genuine Christian doctrine. At that time, the Church was still just emerging, and there were a number of false teachings spreading throughout the churches across the Roman Empire.

In many ways, the Church is experiencing a similar dynamic across the world today. Crazy, off-the-wall doctrines are gaining ground among professing Christians at an alarming rate. We too need the "truth filter" of The Apostles' Creed to help keep us on track and weed out what are and are not genuine Christian beliefs. Here again is The Apostles' Creed in its entirety:

> **I believe in God, the Father Almighty,**
> **the Creator of heaven and earth,**
> **and in Jesus Christ, His only Son, our Lord:**
> **Who was conceived of the Holy Spirit,**
> **born of the Virgin Mary,**
> **suffered under Pontius Pilate,**
> **was crucified, died, and was buried.**
> **He descended into hell.**
> **The third day He arose again from the dead.**
> **He ascended into heaven**
> **and sits at the right hand of God the Father Almighty,**
> **whence He shall come to judge the living and the dead.**
> **I believe in the Holy Spirit,**
> **the holy catholic [universal] church,**
> **the communion of saints,**
> **the forgiveness of sins,**
> **the resurrection of the body,**
> **and life everlasting. Amen.**

In this lesson, we will turn our attention to the fifth main doctrine of the faith — the belief that He [Jesus] was crucified, died, and was buried.

The Horrific Act of Crucifixion

After Jesus stood trial and was examined by Pontius Pilate, He was then brutally scourged and "…[They] led him away to crucify him" (Matthew 27:31). The Bible then adds, "And when they were come unto a place called Golgotha, that is to say, a place of a skull…they crucified him…" (Matthew 27:33,35).

In the First Century, there was no death more wretched and barbaric than death by hanging on the cross. The Greek word for "cross" and "crucified" in the New Testament is *stauros*, and it describes an upright, pointed stake used for the punishment of criminals. It was used to depict those hung up, impaled, beheaded, and publicly displayed, and was always used in connection with public executions. Hanging a criminal publicly was intended to bring ultimate humiliation and punishment to the accused.

Crucifixion was the lowest and most barbaric form of punishment in the ancient world. Noted Jewish historian Flavius Josephus described crucifixion as the most wretched of all deaths. At the time that Jesus was crucified, the act of crucifixion was entirely in the hands of Roman authorities. Ancient writers tell us that Roman soldiers took great pleasure in the act of crucifixion, often crucifying individuals in different positions. This punishment was reserved for the most serious offenders, usually for those who had committed some kind of treason or who had participated in or sponsored state terrorism.

Nails Were Driven Through the Wrists and Feet

Once the offender reached the place where the crucifixion was to occur, he was laid on the crossbeam with arms outstretched. Soldiers would then drive a five-inch iron nail through each of the victim's wrists. It was not through the palm of his hands, but through his wrists and into the crossbeam. If the nail had been driven through the palms, it would have ripped through the flesh.

After being nailed to the crossbeam, the victim was hoisted by a rope, and the crossbeam was dropped into a notch on the top of the upright post. When the crossbeam dropped into the groove, the victim suffered excruciating pain as his hands and wrists were wrenched by the sudden jerking motion. Eventually, the weight of the victim's body caused his arms to be pulled from their sockets.

Once the victim's wrists were secured in place on the crossbeam, the feet came next. The victim's legs would be positioned so that the feet were pointed downward with the soles pressed against the post on which he was suspended. A long nail would then be driven between the bones of the feet. The nail was lodged firmly enough between those bones to prevent it from tearing through the feet as the victim arched upward gasping for breath.

The Process of Asphyxiation

In order for the victim to breathe, he had to push himself up by the feet, which were nailed to the vertical post. But because the pressure in his feet would become unbearable, he could not remain in that position for very long. Eventually, he would collapse back into the hanging position.

As the victim pushed up and collapsed back down again and again over a long period of time, his shoulders eventually dislocated and popped out of joint. Soon afterward, the elbows and wrists would follow. Historians tell us these various dislocations caused the arms to be extended up to nine inches longer than normal, often resulting in terrible cramps in the victim's arm muscles and making it impossible for him to push himself up any longer to breathe. When he was finally too exhausted and could no longer push himself up on the nail lodged in his feet, the process of asphyxiation began.

Jesus experienced all this torture on the Cross. When He dropped down with the full weight of His body on the nails that were driven through His wrists, it sent horrific pain up His arms that registered in His brain. Added to this torture was the agony caused by the constant grating of His back that had just been scourged. Every time He pushed Himself up to breathe and then collapsed back into a hanging position, His back grated against the upright post.

Due to the extreme loss of blood and hyperventilation, a victim would begin to experience severe dehydration. We can see this process in Jesus' own crucifixion when He cried out in John 19:28 and said, "I thirst." After several hours of this torment, the victim's heart would begin to fail. Next his lungs would collapse, and excess fluid would begin filling the lining of his heart and lungs, adding to the slow process of asphyxiation. A person who was crucified eventually drowned as his own fluids filled his lungs.

Jesus Cried, 'It Is Finished!'

When we come to John 19:30, we find some of the most powerful words ever uttered by Jesus: "…He said, *It is finished*: and he bowed his head, and gave up the ghost." In that moment, all the Old Testament prophecies about Jesus' earthly ministry were fulfilled. The justice of God had been fully met in Jesus who died as the Lamb of God to take away the sins of the world.

Jesus' mission was accomplished. Thus, He could cry out that His task was complete! Jesus paid the price for your salvation, for your liberation, for your physical healing, and for your complete restoration.

Jesus Was Verifiably Dead

Joseph and Nicodemus Laid Him To Rest

After six grueling hours on the Cross, the execution was completed, and it was time to take down Jesus' body. It was then that Pilate was secretly visited by a very powerful Jewish leader named Joseph of Arimathea. With fierce urgency, Joseph requested the body of Jesus, and Pilate granted his request. Joseph was then joined by Nicodemus, and the two devoted followers prepared Christ's body for burial, using a 100-pound mixture of myrrh and aloes and a linen cloth.

The Bible says, "Now in the place where he was crucified there was a garden; and in the garden a new sepulchre, wherein was never man yet laid. There laid they Jesus therefore because of the Jews' preparation day; for the sepulchre was nigh at hand" (John 19:41,42).

The word "laid" is important. It is the Greek word *tithimi*, which means *to set*, *to lay*, *to place*, *to deposit*, or *to set in place*. It is used in this verse to describe how Joseph and Nicodemus very carefully placed Jesus' lifeless body in its resting place inside the tomb.

They had spent hours hovering over Him during the process of ceremonially cleansing and wrapping the body of Jesus in 100 pounds of spices. If there had been even a flicker of a pulse or a whisper of breath left in Jesus' lungs, they would have seen it. But there was none. Christ was dead.

The Women Carefully Observed Him

According to Luke's gospel, the men were not alone. Luke 23:55 says, "And the women also, which came with him from Galilee, followed after, and beheld the sepulchre, and how his body was laid." The word "beheld" here is the Greek word *theaomai*, and in this verse it means *to gaze upon, to fully see*, or *to look at intently*. It is where we get the word *theater*.

The use of the word *theaomai* indicates that the women didn't rush in and rush out of the tomb. Instead, they watched every act and movement — as if they were in a theater. With eyes wide open, they inspected "how" Jesus' dead body was laid. The word "how" is the Greek word *hos*, which describes *careful contemplation and very careful observance*. Thus, they intently gazed at the body of Jesus and observed everything about Him. Mark's gospel verifies this in Mark 15:47. The reason the women paused and pondered over Jesus was that they didn't think they would ever see Him again. He was verifiably dead, and this was their final farewell to the One they loved deeply. They wanted to make sure everything was done honorably and correctly.

After Joseph and Nicodemus had carefully laid Jesus' body to rest in the fresh stone tomb and everyone had said goodbye, Matthew 27:60 says, "…He [Joseph] rolled a great stone to the door of the sepulchre, and departed." As far as they were concerned, that was the end.

The Religious Leaders Requested That Jesus' Tomb Be 'Sealed'

Although sorrow gripped the hearts of the disciples, fear gripped the hearts of the religious leaders. They were very concerned that somehow Jesus' disciples would come at night and steal His body and then claim He was resurrected. Matthew 27:62-64 explains:

> **Now the next day, that followed the day of preparation, the chief priests and Pharisees came together unto Pilate, saying, Sir, we remember that that deceiver said while he was yet alive, After three days I will rise again. Command therefore that the sepulchre be made sure until the third day, lest his disciples come by night, and steal him away, and say unto the people, He is risen from the dead; so the last error shall be worse than the first.**

Notice what the religious leaders requested — that Pilate "Command therefore that the sepulchre be made *sure…*" (Matthew 27:64). The word "sure" is the Greek word *sphragidzo*, and it describes *a legal seal placed on documents, letters, and possessions*. In this case, it was *the seal of Pilate being placed upon a tomb*. The purpose of a seal of this nature was to authenticate that the sealed item had been properly inspected before sealing and that all the contents were in order. As long as the seal remained unbroken, it guaranteed that the contents inside were safe, sound, and undisturbed.

These Jewish leaders were asking that a string be stretched across the entrance of the tomb, from one side to the other, and at the end of the string was Pilate's official seal pressed into wax. He was the governor of Judea, and no one was higher in authority than him. Therefore, his seal was very powerful and important. No one had dared break the seal that was put in place by Pontius Pilate.

An Inspection Was Required First

In order for the tomb to be made "sure" (*sphragidzo*) — or officially sealed — the contents inside had to first be checked. For this to happen, the religious leaders, along with Roman soldiers and officials from Pilate's court had to come to the tomb and reopen it. They had to roll away the stone, enter the tomb, and check everything to make sure everything was in order.

Keep in mind, Joseph of Arimathea, Nicodemus, and the women were totally unaware that this was taking place. As far as they knew, they had carefully prepared Jesus' body for burial, laid Him to rest, and sealed the tomb with the large stone.

Nevertheless, Pilate's officials along with the Roman soldiers and members of the Jewish Sanhedrin went to the tomb, rolled back the stone, and went inside to carefully inspect the body of Jesus. They wanted to know that His body was still there and that He was really dead, so that is what they did. Pilate would have never sealed the tomb unless they had first conducted a full inspection and affirmed that Jesus was there and He was dead. As long as the seal remained unbroken, *it guaranteed that the contents inside were safe and sound.*

A Watch Was Then Requested

Even with Pilate's seal in place, the religious leaders still had doubts and fears concerning Jesus' body. Accordingly, they asked for more security. Matthew 27:65 states, "Pilate said unto them, Ye have a watch: go your way, make it as sure as ye can."

The word "watch" in Greek is the word *koustodia*, which describes *a guard or watch*. In the First Century, it pictured *a group of four Roman soldiers whose shift changed every three hours*. The shift frequently rotated to ensure the soldiers were alert and fully awake at all times. When Pilate said, "Ye have a watch," a better translation would be, "Here. I'm giving you a set of soldiers. Take them and guard the tomb."

Also note the word "sure" in verse 65. It is different than the word used in verse 64. Here, the word "sure" is the Greek word *asphalidzo*, which means *to provide added security or to assure that security is achieved*. "So they went, and made the sepulchre sure, sealing the stone, and setting a watch" (Matthew 27:66).

Jesus' Death Was Legally Authenticated

Make no mistake — Jesus Christ was dead. The centurion who thrust his spear into Jesus' side saw the mixture of blood and water flow (*see* John 19:34,35). This was confirmation of congestive heart failure. The centurion verified Jesus was dead and notified Pilate *before* the body was given to Joseph of Arimathea (*see* Mark 15:44,45).

Joseph of Arimathea and Nicodemus spent hours preparing Jesus' body for burial. Mary Magdalene and Mary the mother of Joses were also present, assisting and gazing intently at Him. Clearly, there was no life left in His mangled form. If He had been alive, they would surely have known it.

Furthermore, the religious leaders along with Roman soldiers and officials from Pilate's court all thoroughly examined Jesus' body in the tomb and unequivocally confirmed He was dead. Romans were masters at inflicting death, so they were well able to recognize a lifeless corpse. Once they all verified the body was Jesus' and that He was dead, they rolled the burial stone back in place, and Pilate's representative sealed the tomb with the official seal of the Roman governor.

All these things legally authenticated that Jesus was dead.

But Death Could Not Hold Jesus!

Nevertheless, regardless of all the efforts of the religious leaders and the Roman officials to secure the site and to keep Jesus inside the grave, it was impossible for death to hold Him! Three days after His torturous death, Jesus was gloriously raised back to life — just as He proclaimed He would!

On the day of Pentecost, Peter proclaimed, "…Ye have taken, and by wicked hands have crucified and slain [Jesus]: whom God hath raised up, having loosed the pains of death: because it was not possible that he should be holden of it" (Acts 2:23,24).

Today the tomb in Jerusalem where Jesus was once laid is empty because He arose from the grave! Now He is seated on His throne at the right hand of the Father on High, where He ever lives to make intercession for you and for me (*see* Hebrews 7:25). Praise His matchless Name!

STUDY QUESTIONS

> **Study to shew thyself approved unto God, a workman that needeth not to be ashamed, rightly dividing the word of truth.**
> **— 2 Timothy 2:15**

1. Before Pilate released Jesus' body to Joseph, what does Mark 15:43-45 say he did first? Did you know this happened prior to this lesson?
2. In your own words, explain what had to be done before Pilate's official seal could be placed on Jesus' tomb. What did the seal signify and how did it legally authenticate Jesus' death?
3. Have you ever really stopped to think about what Jesus did for us as He endured such a torturous death on the Cross? Read Galatians 3:13; Romans 8:1-4; Second Corinthians 5:21; and First Peter 2:24 for some of the amazing blessings we've received through His priceless sacrifice.

PRACTICAL APPLICATION

> **But be ye doers of the word, and not hearers only, deceiving your own selves.**
> **— James 1:22**

1. Right after Jesus surrendered His spirit and died, some amazing things took place in the temple and in Jerusalem. Read Matthew 27:51-55 and tell what happened in your own words. If you had been in the temple or wandering around the city and witnessed these events, how do you think you would have reacted?
2. Imagine that you were there with Joseph of Arimathea, Nicodemus, Mary Magdalene, and Mary the mother of Joses to help them prepare Jesus' body for burial. What kind of questions would you be asking? How do you think it would feel to see His body, barely recognizable and no longer breathing? Do you think it would have been any harder to remember His promise to rise again?
3. On that note, what's something God has promised you that looks *dead* right now? Talk to Him about it and take time to grieve the fact that things didn't go the way you hoped and expected. Ask Him to give you hope for your future and for the ability to stay close to Him until you see the fulfillment of His promise. Journal whatever He shows you and take time to receive His comfort.

LESSON 6

TOPIC
He Descended Into Hell

SCRIPTURES
1. **1 Peter 3:19** — By which also he went and preached unto the spirits in prison.
2. **Colossians 2:15** — And having spoiled principalities and powers, he made a shew of them openly, triumphing over them in it.
3. **Ephesians 1:21,22** — Far above all principality, and power, and might, and dominion, and every name that is named, not only in this world, but also in that which is to come: And hath put all things under his feet, and gave him to be the head over all things to the church.

GREEK WORDS

1. "by which" — ἐν ᾧ (*en ho*): in which; points to a significant event that occurred during the time that Christ's physical body laid lifeless in the tomb; could be translated *in which time* or *during which time*
2. "also" — καί (*kai*): additionally or also; used to inform us of additional activity that occurred during the time that Christ's physical body lay lifeless in the earth
3. "went" — πορεύομαι (*poreuomai*): denotes travel through a passageway that enables one to go from one location to another; while it carries the idea of departure, it also means to arrive at a destination; in using this word, Peter was stating that during the time that Christ's physical body lay lifeless in the grave, His spirit departed, traveled to, and arrived at a place that Peter identified as a prison where spirits were held
4. "preached" — κηρύσσω (*kerusso*): to announce, declare, herald, or publish as in the example of a messenger dispatched to announce, declare, herald, or publish a message; the word κηρύσσω (*kerusso*) carries the concept of using speech to unmistakably convey one's authority; Greek writers used this term when describing a court messenger commissioned to read aloud a carefully handed down judgment from a king to his subjects
5. "unto the spirits" — τοῖς πνεύμασιν (*tois pneumasin*): means *to the spirits* and refers *to spirits* held in prison
6. "prison" — φυλακή (*phulake*): a place of custody or a prison that is heavily guarded by keepers and watchmen; denotes a prison chamber in which the most hardened, dangerous, and menacing prisoners were confined and who were accompanied by prison guards who guarded them nonstop
7. "spoiled" — ἀπεκδύομαι (*apekduomai*): to completely strip bare, as in ripping a garment or weapon off someone
8. "principalities" — τὰς ἀρχὰς (*tas archas*): the chief princes or the ruling principalities; referring to dark spiritual powers
9. "powers" — τὰς ἐξουσίας (*tas exousias*): influencing powers
10. "shew" — δειγματίζω (*deigmatidzo*): to expose, to make an example, or to make a public example
11. "openly" — ἐν παρρησίᾳ (*en parresia*): in great boldness; with great frankness; indisputably

12. "triumphing" — θριαμβεύω (*thriambeuo*): to humiliatingly lead a prisoner or prisoners in a victorious triumphal parade
13. "far above" — ὑπεράνω (*huperano*): means high above or far above and refers to both rank and dignity; in the context of this verse, it means quite simply no one in the universe has a higher rank, name, or position than Jesus Christ
14. "all" — πάσης (*pases*): anything and everything
15. "principality" — ἀρχῆς (*arches*): denotes rulers of the highest level; this term refers to all human rulers, including kings and politicians; also used to refer to angelic beings
16. "power" — ἐξουσίας (*exousias*): those who have received delegated power; often translated authorities
17. "might" — δυνάμεως (*dunameos*): explosive power; also used to describe the full strength of a military force
18. "dominion" — κυριότητος (*kuriotetos*): lordships; refers to any world system, political, financial, or a system of any type
19. "under" — ὑποτάσσω (*hupotasso*): a military term meaning to subjugate or to dominate

SYNOPSIS

Did you know that the original 12 apostles believed that Jesus *descended into hell*? It's true, and they felt it was so important that they included it as one of the major tenets of the Christian faith in The Apostles' Creed. Although there are a number of professing Christians who strongly disagree with this teaching, it is a fact that is based on the Holy Scriptures. Why did Jesus descend into hell, and what happened while He was there? Answers to these and other questions are in this sixth lesson.

The emphasis of this lesson:

During the three days that Christ's body lay dead in the tomb, His spirit descended into hell where He announced God's judgment to the evil spirits imprisoned there. He also stripped the enemy of all his weaponry and boldly humiliated every evil power gathered against us. In a triumphal procession, Jesus paraded the defeated enemy for all to see. Our Savior now holds the highest rank of authority in the universe.

A Quick Review of The Apostles' Creed

What we now call The Apostles' Creed dates back to approximately 140 AD in its oldest form, which was earlier known as The Old Roman Creed. The version we have today likely dates to approximately 390 AD. Early Church fathers referred to The Apostles' Creed as "the rule of faith," and it is a condensed compilation of the teachings of the apostles — thus the reason it is referred to as The Apostles' Creed.

This historic creed covers the unchallengeable, core beliefs of the Christian faith, and in the centuries that followed, The Apostles' Creed was used like a "truth filter" to determine what was and wasn't genuine Christian doctrine. Today, The Apostles' Creed is still widely used in denominations all over the world where congregations of all kinds quote these truths with great confidence and faith. Although there's room for dialogue on other principles of the Christian faith, these truths are nonnegotiable.

Here again is The Apostles' Creed:

**I believe in God, the Father Almighty,
the Creator of heaven and earth,
and in Jesus Christ, His only Son, our Lord:
Who was conceived of the Holy Spirit,
born of the Virgin Mary,
suffered under Pontius Pilate,
was crucified, died, and was buried.
He descended into hell.
The third day He arose again from the dead.
He ascended into heaven
and sits at the right hand of God the Father Almighty,
whence He shall come to judge the living and the dead.
I believe in the Holy Spirit,
the holy catholic [universal] church,
the communion of saints,**

the forgiveness of sins,
the resurrection of the body,
and life everlasting. Amen.

Peter Said 'Additional Activity' Took Place While Jesus' Body Lay Dead in the Tomb

When Jesus was hanging on the Cross, He absorbed into His body the sin of all humanity, and when He died, God put sin to death in Christ. The apostle Peter told us one of the things Jesus did between His physical death and resurrection. He said, "By which also he went and preached unto the spirits in prison" (1 Peter 3:19).

Notice the words "by which." They are a translation of the Greek words *en ho*, and they point to a significant event that occurred during the time that Christ's physical body lay lifeless in the tomb. These two words could be translated *in which time* or *during which time*, which means that while Jesus' body lay silent in Joseph of Arimathea's grave, His spirit descended into the abyss of hell.

Even the word "also" is important. It is the Greek word *kai*, meaning *additionally* or *also*. It is used to inform us of *additional activity* that occurred during the time that Christ's physical body lay lifeless in the earth. Hence, in addition to Jesus' crucifixion and burial, *additional activity took place during the time* His body was in the tomb.

Jesus 'Preached to Spirits in Prison'

What was this additional activity that took place while Jesus' body was in the tomb? The Bible says, "…He [Jesus] went and preached unto the spirits in prison" (1 Peter 3:19). The word "went" is a form of the Greek word *poreuomai*, and it denotes *travel through a passageway that enables one to go from one location to another*. It carries the idea of *departure*, and at the same time it also means *to arrive at a destination*. By using this word, Peter was stating that during the time that Christ's physical body lay lifeless in the grave, His spirit departed, traveled to, and arrived at a place that Peter identified as *a prison where spirits were held*.

This brings us to the word "preached," which is a form of the Greek word *kerusso*, meaning *to announce, declare, herald*, or *publish* as in the example of a messenger dispatched to announce, declare, herald, or publish a message.

This word *kerusso* — translated here as "preached" — carries the concept of *using speech to unmistakably convey one's authority*. Greek writers used this term when describing a court messenger commissioned to read aloud a carefully handed down judgment from a king to his subjects.

In this case, Christ announced God's judgment "unto the spirits." This phrase is a translation of the Greek words *tois pneumasin*, which means *to the spirits* and refers *to spirits held in prison*. Under the inspiration of the Holy Spirit, Peter informed us that Jesus boldly approached spirits — likely the fallen angels — who sowed rebellion into the human race during the times of Noah. These were the angels who co-habited with women and produced a hybrid race of giants (*see* Genesis 6:1-13). Peter said that Christ literally went to the compartments of hell (the Greek word *Tartaros*) where these evil "spirits" — plural — were incarcerated, and He peered directly into their nefarious eyes and proclaimed their judgment and the victory of God Almighty over them.

The Greek word for "prison" here is *phulake*, which describes *a place of custody or a prison that is heavily guarded by keepers and watchmen*. Specifically, it denotes *a prison chamber in which the most hardened, dangerous, and menacing prisoners were confined and who were accompanied by prison guards who guarded them nonstop*.

Taking into account the original Greek meaning of all these words, here is the *Renner Interpretive Version (RIV)* of First Peter 3:19:

> **But during the time [that His body was dead], He additionally also departed and journeyed all the way to a dreadful prison in which hardened, dangerous, and menacing spirits were confined and guarded….**

Jesus Stripped the Enemy of All His Weapons

After informing us that our transgressions were blotted out and nailed to the Cross with Christ, the apostle Paul went on to say, "And having spoiled principalities and powers, he [Jesus] made a shew of them openly, triumphing over them in it" (Colossians 2:15). To get a better grasp of what Christ accomplished, let's unpack the original meaning of this verse starting with the word *spoiled*.

In Greek, the word "spoiled" is *apekduomai*, which means *to completely strip bare*, as in *ripping a garment or weapon off someone* or *taking their weapons away* from them. In this instance, it refers to Jesus stripping the enemy bare of all his weaponry. The Bible describes the enemy as *principalities* and *powers*.

The word "principalities" in Greek is *tas archas*, and it denotes *the chief princes* or *the ruling principalities*, referring to *dark spiritual powers*. The word "powers" is a translation of the Greek words *tas exousias*, which describes *influencing powers*. Scripture says that Jesus stripped the chief ruling princes and the dark, influencing powers of all their weaponry and "made a shew of them openly."

Jesus Boldly Humiliated the Evil Powers Arrayed Against Us

This strange word "shew" is a form of the Greek word *deigmatidzo*, which means *to expose, to make an example*, or *to make a public example*. Thus, through Jesus' death on the Cross, He *openly* humiliated all the evil powers and principalities that were gathered against us. The word "openly" is a translation of the Greek phrase *en parresia*, which means *in great boldness*; *with great frankness*; or *indisputably*.

Keep in mind, Paul painted a picture of what Jesus did through His crucifixion. In addition to taking the punishment for our sin, He descended into hell while His body lay in the grave, and in hell, He irrefutably triumphed over all the powers of darkness, boldly making a humiliating example of them.

This brings us to the word "triumphing," which is a form of the Greek word *thriambeuo*, meaning *to humiliatingly lead a prisoner or prisoners in a victorious triumphal parade*. This is a technical word used to describe *a general* or *an emperor returning home from a grand victory in the enemy's territory*. Specifically, the word *thriambeuo* (triumphing) denoted the emperor's triumphal parade when he returned home.

When a returning emperor or general came striding through the gates on his powerful and beautiful horse, he was accompanied by his fellow victorious warriors who appeared glorious after their triumphant battle. As the parade followed, the weaponry and treasures seized from the enemy's territory were grandly displayed for all to see.

The Devil and His Forces Were Disgraced and Defeated

The grand finale to this triumphal procession was the conquered foreign ruler himself. He had been beaten and bound in chains and was now being forced to walk in disgrace, shame, dishonor, embarrassment, and humiliation as crowds of people came to celebrate his defeat and to get a peek at a once-powerful but now totally defeated foe.

So when Colossians 2:15 declares that Jesus triumphed over evil powers, it is explicitly proclaiming that Jesus took the enemy apart piece by piece as He thoroughly "spoiled principalities and powers." Thus, when Jesus was finished with these demonic forces, they were *utterly plundered — "stripped to bare nakedness" and left with nothing in hand to retaliate!*

Taking into account the Greek meaning of the words *en parresia* and *triumbeuo*, here is the *Renner Interpretive Version (RIV)* of Colossians 2:15:

> …**He [Jesus] gallantly strode into Heaven to celebrate His victory and the defeat of Satan and his forces. As part of His triumphal process, He flaunted the spoils seized from the hand of the enemy. Yet the greatest spectacle of all occurred when the enemy himself was openly put on display as bound, disgraced, disabled, defeated, humiliated, and stripped bare.…**

This passage tells us unequivocally that Jesus' victory over Satan was a momentous affair! When Jesus returned, He was totally triumphant! The party that Heaven threw that day was enormous! All of Heaven's hosts came to celebrate Jesus' victory and Satan's downfall and demise! Right there in front of everyone, Jesus displayed the devil and his cohorts, so all could know that this enemy no longer had the legitimate right or the necessary weapons to prolong his rule of terrorism.

What Are the Results of Jesus' Victory?

As a result of Christ's irrefutable defeat of the devil and his foes, the Bible says God has exalted Him "Far above all principality, and power, and might, and dominion, and every name that is named, not only in this world, but also in that which is to come" (Ephesians 1:21).

Interestingly, the words "far above" are translated from the Greek word *huperano*, which means *high above* or *far above* and refers to both *rank* and *dignity*. In the context of this verse, it means quite simply *no one in the universe has a higher rank, name, or position than Jesus Christ!* To affirm that Jesus holds this highest position, Paul added the word "all," which is the Greek word *pases*, describing *anything and everything*. When the words *huperano* and *pases* are used together, it leaves no room for misunderstanding or doubt regarding his message:

> **Jesus Christ holds the highest and most exalted position in the entire universe; He is literally "above all."**

Paul then went on to describe the specific categories that Christ is *above all*.

Christ is far above all "principality." This is the Greek word *arches*, and it denotes *rulers of the highest level*. Although this term refers to *all human rulers*, including *kings* and *politicians*, it is also used to refer to *angelic beings*. Thus, Jesus' exalted rank is above all human rulers and all supernatural beings alike. There is no one in the physical or spiritual realm that holds a higher rank than Christ.

Christ is far above all "power." The Greek word for "power" here is *exousias*, and it describes *those who have received delegated power* and is often translated *authorities*. In this verse, it refers to *people who hold public office and wield authority entrusted to them by their superiors or through an election*. Essentially, what Paul was teaching is that although these individuals yield substantial power and influence in the affairs of the world, their authority pales in comparison to that of Jesus Christ. He is far above them all!

At the time Paul penned these words in the First Century AD, this was a very dangerous and powerful statement to make, because Roman political powers were actively persecuting the Church and attempting to suppress the message of the Gospel. Nevertheless, Paul wanted his readers to know that no matter what authority a politician might try to exert over the Church, Jesus had a rank that was even higher than any powerful human authority.

Christ is far above all "might." The Greek word for "might" here is *dunameos*, which depicts *explosive power*. It is also used to describe *the full strength of a military force*. The use of this word tells us that Jesus is far above all the military forces in the world.

Christ is far above all "dominion." The word "dominion" is a translation of the Greek word *kuriotetos*, which means *lordship* and can refer to *any* *world system — political, financial,* or *a system of any type.* There simply is no system more high-ranking than the Lord Jesus Christ!

Christ is far above "every name." Finally, Paul added that Christ is far above "…every name that is named, not only in this world, but also in that which is to come" (Ephesians 1:21). In one sweeping statement, Paul declared that Jesus is Lord over all.

- He is literally superior to all rulers (*arches*) — including ruling spiritual forces.
- He is far above all elected leaders (*exousias*).
- He is far above all military powers (*dunameos*).
- He is far above all constitutional authorities (*kuriotes*) — any world system of any kind.

Jesus is literally Lord over all!

All Things Are Under Jesus' Feet!

In Paul's next breath, he declared that God "…hath put all things under his [Christ's] feet, and gave him to be the head over all things to the church" (Ephesians 1:22). The word "under" here is the Greek word *hupotasso*, a military term meaning *to subjugate or to dominate*. It described forcibly subduing a conquered people and putting them in their place.

Paul's use of this word in Ephesians 1:22 is not figurative or symbolic. Jesus Christ — through His death on the Cross, descent into hell, resurrection, and ascension on High — literally put every foe that ever existed under His feet. Nothing and no one in the universe is more highly exalted than Jesus Christ. His throne rules above all — above all human authorities, military authorities, and spiritual authorities. There is simply no one who rules higher or more majestically than Jesus.

In our next lesson, we'll look at the next major pillar of the Christian faith: The third day Jesus arose from the dead.

STUDY QUESTIONS

> **Study to shew thyself approved unto God, a workman that needeth not to be ashamed, rightly dividing the word of truth.**
> **— 2 Timothy 2:15**

1. Although some argue that Jesus didn't descend into hell, the Bible speaks plainly that He did. Consider these passages and write how each confirms this statement of faith to be true.
   - Matthew 12:38,39; Luke 11:29,30
   - Acts 2:30,31
   - Ephesians 4:7-10
   - Revelation 1:18
2. Take a few minutes to reread First Peter 3:19 and its meaning in Greek. Had you heard this verse before? What is God showing you in it, and how does it help you better understand what Jesus was doing while His body was in the tomb?
3. Reread the sections explaining the meaning of Colossians 2:15. What new insights is the Holy Spirit revealing to you about Christ's victory over Satan? How does this understanding expand the meaning of Jesus' words in Luke 10:19 and Paul's words in Romans 8:31,32 and Second Corinthians 2:14?

PRACTICAL APPLICATION

> But be ye doers of the word, and not hearers only, deceiving your own selves.
> —James 1:22

1. When you hear the truth that no one in the universe — in the natural or spiritual realm — has a higher rank, name, or position than Jesus Christ, how does it encourage you?
2. Ephesians 1:21 says that Jesus holds a rank that is "Far above all principality, and power, and might, and dominion…." In your own words, describe the meaning of each of these categories of rulers over which Jesus is superior.
   - Principality _____
   - Power _____
   - Might _____
   - Dominion _____

3. The Bible declares that God "…hath put all things under his [Christ's] feet…" (Ephesians 1:22). If you are *in Christ*, what does this say about "all things" that come against you?

LESSON 7

TOPIC
The Third Day He Rose From the Dead

SCRIPTURES

1. **Matthew 28:1,2** — In the end of the sabbath, as it began to dawn toward the first day of the week, came Mary Magdalene and the other Mary to see the sepulchre. And, behold, there was a great earthquake: for the angel of the Lord descended from heaven, and came and rolled back the stone from the door, and sat upon it.
2. **Mark 16:2-4** — And very early in the morning the first day of the week, they came unto the sepulchre at the rising of the sun. And they said among themselves, Who shall roll us away the stone from the door of the sepulchre? And when they looked, they saw that the stone was rolled away: for it was very great.
3. **Matthew 28:4** — And for fear of him the keepers did shake, and became as dead men.
4. **Luke 24:3-9** — And they entered in, and found not the body of the Lord Jesus. And it came to pass, as they were much perplexed thereabout, behold, two men stood by them in shining garments: And as they were afraid, and bowed down their faces to the earth, they said unto them, Why seek ye the living among the dead? He is not here, but is risen: remember how he spake unto you when he was yet in Galilee, saying, The Son of man must be delivered into the hands of sinful men, and be crucified, and the third day rise again. And they remembered his words, And returned from the sepulchre, and told all these things unto the eleven, and to all the rest.
5. **Matthew 28:8** — And they departed quickly from the sepulchre with fear and great joy; and did run to bring his disciples word.

6. **John 20:3-6,8** — Peter therefore went forth, and that other disciple, and came to the sepulchre. So they ran both together: and the other disciple did outrun Peter, and came first to the sepulchre. And he stooping down, and looking in, saw the linen clothes lying; yet went he not in. Then cometh Simon Peter following him, and went into the sepulchre, and seeth the linen clothes lie… Then went in also that other disciple, which came first to the sepulchre, and he saw, and believed.

GREEK WORDS
No Greek words were shown on the TV program.

SYNOPSIS
Many people love the Christmas story, which centers around the birth of Jesus in Bethlehem more than 2,000 years ago. Certainly, the Lord's birth is reason to celebrate, but it would be meaningless without His crucifixion and, most importantly, His resurrection. Indeed, the resurrection of Jesus Christ from the dead is the foundation of the Christian faith. When the power of God exploded inside the tomb, it flooded Jesus' corpse with life, reconnecting His spirit with His physical body. In that moment, Jesus arose! This is no legend or fairy tale — it is the centerpiece of the Gospel and a vital part of The Apostles' Creed.

The emphasis of this lesson:

Matthew, Mark, Luke, and John all record events that took place on the morning of Christ's resurrection. The massive stone was rolled away, the earth quaked, and Jesus came back to life! The Roman guards were petrified at the angel's appearance, but the women who devotedly followed Jesus were filled with new hope at the news of His resurrection.

What We Know Without Question Is Going To Happen In the Last of the Last Days

The Holy Spirit, speaking through the apostle Paul, prophetically pointed His finger 2,000 years into the future and told us what would take place. Paul said, "Now the Spirit speaketh expressly, that in the latter times some shall depart from the faith, giving heed to seducing spirits, and doctrines of devils" (1 Timothy 4:1).

Notice it says the Spirit "speaketh expressly." These words are a translation of the Greek word *rhetos*, and it describes *something that is emphatic, categorical*, and *unmistakable*. It pictures *something spoken clearly* or *something that is unquestionable, certain*, and *sure*. In other words, this is not something that *might* happen but something that will most emphatically and assuredly happen.

Also notice *when* this is going to take place: the Spirit said in the "latter times." The word "latter" is the Greek word *husteros*, which means *later*, and it pictures *the ultimate end or the very last of something*. Moreover, the word "times" is the Greek word *kairos*, describing *a season*. By using these words, the Holy Spirit is telling us that something most definitely is going to happen at the very end of the Church age — a season when there is virtually no more time remaining.

What does the Spirit say is surely going to come to pass? He said, "…Some shall depart from the faith…" (1 Timothy 4:1). The word *some* indicates that not everyone is going to depart, but only *some* — a Greek word which describes *a notable some* or *a substantial number of people*.

This brings us to the word "depart," which is the Greek word *aphistemi*, a compound of the words *apo* and *histimi*. The word *apo* means *away*, and the word *histimi* means *to stand*. When these words are joined to form *aphistemi*, the new word means *to stand apart from; to distance one's self from; to step away from; to withdraw from;* or *to shrink away from*. It is the very Greek word that we derive the word "apostate" or "apostasy."

The use of this word *aphistemi* does not describe an outright rejection of the faith — it describes a very slow, methodical withdrawal or stepping away from the faith. In fact, it is so slow that those who are in transition may not even realize they're moving. Nevertheless, a certain number of people will release what they once believed and move in another direction. The fact that Paul says it is "the faith" lets us know that this is *not* faith for miracles, faith for healing, faith for finances, or faith for anything else. This is *THE faith*, meaning the clear, time-tested truth of God's eternal Word.

Why will some believers depart from the faith? The Holy Spirit said they will be "…giving heed to seducing spirits, and doctrines of devils" (1 Timothy 4:1). The word "seducing" here is a form of the Greek word *planao*, which means *to wander* and describes *a moral wandering*. It is a picture of a person (or nation) that has veered from a solid path, and as a result of veering morally, this person is off track.

The word "doctrines" is also very important. It is the Greek word *didaskalia*, and it describes *a well-packaged teaching that is applicable to a lifestyle*. Thus, when the teaching is presented, the deception sounds logical and appeals to one's flesh. This tells us that the devil is not going to show up in a red suit with a pitchfork in his hand and horns on his head. He's going to come with what sounds sensible and logical, but it is a progressive, new way of thinking that will lure people away from the foundation of the truth of Scripture.

We're living in this age of deception. What's very interesting is that every time the Bible talks about the coming of the Lord, it is paralleled with a conversation about deception. At the time of Jesus' return, deception will be at an all-time high world-wide. Again, that's the age in which we're living.

Knowing that people will be lured away from the foundation of God's Word, we need to be established in truth. A careful study of The Apostles' Creed helps ensure that we're on a solid foundation. Here again is The Apostles' Creed:

> **I believe in God, the Father Almighty,**
> **the Creator of heaven and earth,**
> **and in Jesus Christ, His only Son, our Lord:**
> **Who was conceived of the Holy Spirit,**
> **born of the Virgin Mary,**
> **suffered under Pontius Pilate,**
> **was crucified, died, and was buried.**
> **He descended into hell.**
> **The third day He arose again from the dead.**
> **He ascended into heaven**
> **and sits at the right hand of God the Father Almighty,**
> **whence He shall come to judge the living and the dead.**
> **I believe in the Holy Spirit,**
> **the holy catholic [universal] church,**
> **the communion of saints,**
> **the forgiveness of sins,**
> **the resurrection of the body,**
> **and life everlasting. Amen.**

The Women Who Attended Jesus Didn't Know the Tomb Had Been Legally Sealed

Matthew, Mark, Luke, and John all record the events that took place on the morning of Christ's resurrection. To begin our focus on this vital topic, we will first turn our attention to Matthew 28:1, which says, "In the end of the sabbath, as it began to dawn toward the first day of the week, came Mary Magdalene and the other Mary to see the sepulchre."

Interestingly, Luke 23:55 and 56 says some of these same women were present when Jesus was placed inside the tomb — and that they *gazed upon* the body of Jesus, inspecting it, and making sure that everything had been done honorably and properly. They saw that His corpse was really there and watched as the doorway was sealed with a massive stone. They then went home to prepare "spices and ointments" so they could anoint His body for burial when they returned.

Think about it: These women had no way of knowing that the chief priests and elders had gone to Pilate after Jesus was buried to request a watch of four Roman soldiers to guard the tomb — or that officials from the Roman court had "sealed" the tomb. Remember, the religious leaders were afraid that Jesus' disciples would come and steal His body. Therefore, they requested that Pilate seal it and give them a group of soldiers that would stand guard at the grave.

Scripture tells us that Pilate granted the request of the religious leaders, and representatives were sent with them to roll back the stone and inspect the contents of the tomb. Once inside, Pilate's delegates, the Roman soldiers, and the religious leaders all saw Jesus' dead body and made sure that everything was in place. They then rolled the stone back in place and officially sealed it.

Had the women known that the tomb was legally sealed and couldn't be opened, they wouldn't have returned to the tomb. Legally it was impossible for them to request the stone to be removed.

The Removal of the Stone and the Earthquake Happened Simultaneously

Similarly, Mark's gospel says, "And very early in the morning the first day of the week, they came unto the sepulchre at the rising of the sun. And they said among themselves, Who shall roll us away the stone from the door of the sepulchre? And when they looked, they saw that the stone was rolled away: for it was very great" (Mark 16:2-4).

Again, we see that the women were ignorant of the fact that the tomb had been sealed by the Roman government and couldn't legally be opened. If they had known, they would have never proceeded to the tomb for the purpose of anointing Jesus' body. As they drew near to where the tomb was located, they talked among themselves, wondering who would remove the stone for them. But when they arrived, the stone was already rolled away.

Looking back at Matthew's account, he documented, "And, behold, there was a great earthquake…" (Matthew 28:2). Amazingly, this great earthquake occurred simultaneously with Jesus' resurrection — before the women arrived at the garden tomb. The word "great" suggests *something huge*, *massive*, or *enormous*. The Greek word for "earthquake" is the word *seismos*, which is the word used today for a literal *earthquake*. The earthquake and the stone being rolled away happened simultaneously.

Mark 16:4 says that when the women arrived at the tomb, they found "…the stone was rolled away: for it was very great." The word "very" here means *very*, *exceedingly*, or *extremely*, and the word "great" is the word *mega*, meaning *huge*, *massive*, or *enormous*. In other words, this was not a normal stone. Yet when the women arrived it was removed!

How was the massive stone removed? Matthew 28:2 says, "…For the angel of the Lord descended from heaven, and came and rolled back the stone from the door, and sat upon it."

How Did the Roman Soldiers and Women Respond to All These Events?

Matthew tells us the response of the soldiers to the angel's appearance. He said, "And for fear of him [the angel] the keepers did shake, and became as dead men" (Matthew 28:4). Just imagine: these mighty Roman soldiers "became as dead men." In Greek, the words "dead men" are translated from the term meaning *a corpse*. The soldiers were so terrified at the appearance of the angel and the divine power he manifested that they fell to the ground as if they were dead, unable to move. When they were finally able to regain their composure, the guards fled the scene.

Meanwhile, Luke tells us that once the stone was removed, the women crossed the threshold into the tomb, "And they entered in, and found not the body of the Lord Jesus" (Luke 24:3). As you might imagine, "…They were much perplexed thereabout…" (Luke 24:4). Clearly, they were perplexed because they came expecting to see the stone in front of the tomb, but it was removed. Immediately, their minds began whirling as to where Jesus was.

Luke then adds, "…Behold, two men stood by them in shining garments: And as they were afraid, and bowed down their faces to the earth, they [the angels] said unto them, Why seek ye the living among the dead? He is not here, but is risen: remember how he spake unto you when he was yet in Galilee, saying, The Son of man must be delivered into the hands of sinful men, and be crucified, and the third day rise again. And they remembered his words" (Luke 24:4-8).

The two angels proclaimed the joyful news of Jesus' resurrection and told the women that Jesus was alive. Matthew 28:8 says, "And they [the women] departed quickly from the sepulchre with fear and great joy; and did run to bring his disciples word." Luke 24:9 confirms this fact, saying that the women "…returned from the sepulchre, and told all these things unto the eleven, and to all the rest."

John and Peter's Reaction to News of the Resurrection

When we look at John's gospel, we get the perspective of how he and Peter responded to the women's report of Christ's resurrection. John said, "Peter therefore went forth, and that other disciple [John], and came to the sepulchre. So they ran both together: and the other disciple [John] did outrun Peter, and came first to the sepulchre" (John 20:3,4).

Although John outran Peter to the garden tomb location, as soon as John arrived, he stopped at the doorway out of great respect. John 20:5 says, "And he stooping down, and looking in, saw the linen clothes lying; yet went he not in." Verse 6 goes on to say, "Then cometh Simon Peter following him, and went into the sepulchre, and seeth the linen clothes lie." Once Peter was inside, "…Then went in also that other disciple, which came first to the sepulchre, and he saw, and believed" (John 20:8).

When Peter and John went into the tomb, they saw the place where the Lord had been carefully laid by Joseph of Arimathea and Nicodemus (*see* John 19:40,41). It was the same place where the women had seen

Christ's body lay and had examined him to make sure everything was in order. It was also the very place where the chief priests and the scribes came to verify that Jesus was really dead and His corpse was secured safely inside the tomb.

But now the stone had been rolled away from the front of the tomb, and Pilate's official seal had been broken. The women had already seen that the tomb was empty, come face to face with an angel, and heard the angels' news that Jesus had been raised from the dead. In that surreal moment, Peter and John were in the tomb and saw for themselves that Jesus was gone, and the Bible says they *believed*.

Later that evening, Jesus would appear to all the apostles (except for Thomas) as they were gathered in the Upper Room. Knowing they were afraid of the Jews, Jesus told them, "…Peace be unto you" (John 20:19). Moments later, the Bible says, "…He breathed on them, and saith unto them, Receive ye the Holy Ghost" (John 20:22). Instantly, the Holy Spirit moved into the hearts of the apostles, and they became the first bornagain people in history.

Friend, Jesus' resurrection is not a hoax or a fairy tale. He really died and He really was raised back to life and came out of that tomb! In our next lesson, we will examine the next statement of faith — that Jesus ascended into Heaven.

STUDY QUESTIONS

Study to shew thyself approved unto God, a workman that needeth not to be ashamed, rightly dividing the word of truth.
— 2 Timothy 2:15

1. What new details did you learn about the events that took place the day of Jesus' resurrection?
2. Matthew provides us with extraordinary facts about the death and resurrection of Jesus that are not found in any other gospel. Take a few moments to read Matthew 28:1-15 and identify the details concerning these events.
   - What amazing things took place immediately after Jesus' died? How did the Roman centurion and those with him react? (*See* Matthew 27:50-56.)

- How did the soldiers at the tomb respond when the angel appeared? (*See* Matthew 28:2-4.)
- What did the angel do and say? Who did he speak to, and who was around? (*See* vv. 2-7.)
- What did the soldiers do when the women (and the angel) left? (*See* vv. 11-15.)

3. It's interesting to note that the angel told the women, "He [Jesus] is not here: for he is risen, *as he said*…" (Matthew 28:6). Did you ever stop to think of how many times Jesus told His disciples that He was going to suffer, die, and be raised back to life? Consider these scripture passages: Matthew 16:21-23; 17:22,23; 26:1,2; Mark 8:31-33; Luke 9:22; 17:25. Why do you think it was so difficult for the disciples to grasp this from Jesus?

PRACTICAL APPLICATION

> But be ye doers of the word, and not hearers only, deceiving your own selves.
> —James 1:22

1. The Holy Spirit informs us that in the last of the last days, a notable number of believers will gradually withdraw and step away from the solid truth of Scripture. In what ways are you personally witnessing this "departure from the faith" in the world today? Who do you know in your sphere of relationships who was once on fire for God, but is now embracing twisted, ungodly ideas?

2. How is this study of The Apostles' Creed helping to ground you in the truth and guard you from the last days apostasy the Holy Spirit prophesied would come?

3. Take a few moments to read Paul's important words in First Corinthians 15:3-7. What tenets of the faith does he include in his encapsulation of the Gospel? And who does he document that Jesus appeared to during the 40 days after His resurrection? Why is this so important for us to know as believers? (For more on who Jesus appeared to after His resurrection, *see* Mark 16:9; Matthew 28:9; Luke 24:15,36; John 20:19,26; and 21:1; and Matthew 28:17.)

LESSON 8

TOPIC
He Ascended Into Heaven

SCRIPTURES

1. **Mark 16:14-20** — Afterward he appeared unto the eleven as they sat at meat.... And he said unto them, Go ye into all the world, and preach the gospel to every creature. He that believeth and is baptized shall be saved; but he that believeth not shall be damned. And these signs shall follow them that believe; In my name shall they cast out devils; they shall speak with new tongues; They shall take up serpents; and if they drink any deadly thing, it shall not hurt them; they shall lay hands on the sick, and they shall recover. So then after the Lord had spoken unto them, he was received up into heaven, and sat on the right hand of God. And they went forth, and preached every where, the Lord working with them, and confirming the word with signs following. Amen.

2. **Luke 24:49-53** — And, behold, I send the promise of my Father upon you: but tarry ye in the city of Jerusalem, until ye be endued with power from on high. And he led them out as far as to Bethany, and he lifted up his hands, and blessed them. And it came to pass, while he blessed them, he was parted from them, and carried up into heaven. And they worshipped him, and returned to Jerusalem with great joy: And were continually in the temple, praising and blessing God. Amen.

3. **Acts 1:6-11** — When they therefore were come together, they asked of him, saying, Lord, wilt thou at this time restore again the kingdom to Israel? And he said unto them, It is not for you to know the times or the seasons, which the Father hath put in his own power. But ye shall receive power, after that the Holy Ghost is come upon you: and ye shall be witnesses unto me both in Jerusalem, and in all Judaea, and in Samaria, and unto the uttermost part of the earth. And when he had spoken these things, while they beheld, he was taken up; and a cloud received him out of their sight. And while they looked stedfastly toward heaven as he went up, behold, two men stood by them in white apparel; Which also said, Ye men of Galilee, why stand ye

gazing up into heaven? this same Jesus, which is taken up from you into heaven, shall so come in like manner as ye have seen him go into heaven.

4. **Matthew 28:16-20** — Then the eleven disciples went away into Galilee, into a mountain where Jesus had appointed them. And when they saw him, they worshipped him: but some doubted. And Jesus came and spake unto them, saying, All power is given unto me in heaven and in earth. Go ye therefore, and teach all nations, baptizing them in the name of the Father, and of the Son, and of the Holy Ghost: Teaching them to observe all things whatsoever I have commanded you: and, lo, I am with you always, even unto the end of the world. Amen.

GREEK WORDS

1. "world" — κόσμος (*kosmos*): the world; also depicts anything fashioned or ordered; denotes systems and institutions in society, such as fashion, education, or entertainment; world systems; often used to denote a particular political system; systems in any part of society

SYNOPSIS

After Christ was gloriously resurrected back to life, the Bible says, "During the forty days after he suffered and died, he appeared to the apostles from time to time, and he proved to them in many ways that he was actually alive. And he talked to them about the Kingdom of God" (Acts 1:3 *NLT*). At the end of those forty days, the gospels of Mark and Luke as well as the book of Acts all document that Jesus ascended back into Heaven. This is a major principle of the Christian faith that was witnessed and believed by the apostles and preserved in The Apostles' Creed.

The emphasis of this lesson:

The gospels of Mark and Luke, along with the book of Acts, record that Jesus physically ascended into Heaven. Just before He left, He told His disciples and His followers to wait in Jerusalem for the empowering gift of the Holy Spirit. He then gave all of us the Great Commission — to make sharing the Gospel a way of life.

A Brief Review of The Apostles' Creed

As we've noted, The Apostles' Creed dates back to approximately 140 AD in its oldest form, and it was earlier known as The Old Roman Creed. But its present form likely dates to approximately 390 AD. It is a condensed compilation of the teachings of the apostles, and hence, the reason it is referred to as The Apostles' Creed. Early Church fathers referred to it as "the rule of faith," as it covers the indisputable core beliefs of the Christian faith. In the centuries that followed, The Apostles' Creed was used like a "truth filter" to determine what was and wasn't genuine Christian doctrine, and it is still widely used today in denominations all over the world. Here again is The Apostles' Creed:

> **I believe in God, the Father Almighty,**
> **the Creator of heaven and earth,**
> **and in Jesus Christ, His only Son, our Lord:**
> **Who was conceived of the Holy Spirit,**
> **born of the Virgin Mary,**
> **suffered under Pontius Pilate,**
> **was crucified, died, and was buried.**
> **He descended into hell.**
> **The third day He arose again from the dead.**
> **He ascended into heaven**
> **and sits at the right hand of God the Father Almighty,**
> **whence He shall come to judge the living and the dead.**
> **I believe in the Holy Spirit,**
> **the holy catholic [universal] church,**
> **the communion of saints,**
> **the forgiveness of sins,**
> **the resurrection of the body,**
> **and life everlasting. Amen.**

'I Believe… [Jesus] Ascended Into Heaven'

The Bible says repeatedly in both the Old and New Testaments, "…The facts of every case must be established by the testimony of two or three witnesses" (2 Corinthians 13:1 *NLT*). Accordingly, Jesus' ascension into Heaven is verified by multiple eyewitnesses and recorded in at least three places in Scripture.

Jesus' Last Words and His Ascension According to Mark's Gospel

First, we turn our attention to Mark's gospel, which is actually Peter's gospel that he dictated to John Mark who served as his secretary. Here the Bible says, "Afterward he [Jesus] appeared unto the eleven as they sat at meat…. And he said unto them, Go ye into all the world, and preach the gospel to every creature" (Mark 16:14,15). The word "world" here is the Greek word *kosmos*, which describes the *world*, but it also depicts *anything fashioned or ordered*. Thus, it denotes *systems and institutions in society*, such as *fashion, education, the judicial system*, or *entertainment*. It includes all kinds of world systems and is often used to denote *a particular political system*.

By using this word *kosmos* — translated here as "world" — Jesus wasn't just saying go into every nation. Rather, He was instructing us to *invade every world system*. This includes the fashion industry, the education system, the judicial system, the political system, the world of entertainment, and every other system of society. We are to go into every single place and share the Gospel to every creature. This is God's command.

What will happen as a result of our "going"? Jesus said, "He that believeth and is baptized shall be saved; but he that believeth not shall be damned" (Mark 16:16). Ironically, many people today — including many Christians — do not believe that those who reject Christ will go to hell. They mistakenly focus solely on God being a God of love and dismiss hell as a made-up fairy tale. Sadly, they overlook the fact that Jesus Himself taught about hell numerous times and clearly said that those "…that believeth not shall be damned." May God give us His heart for the lost so that we share the truth of the Gospel with those who don't know Him.

Jesus went on to say:

And these signs shall follow them that believe; In my name shall they cast out devils; they shall speak with new tongues; They shall take up serpents; and if they drink any deadly thing, it shall not hurt them; they shall lay hands on the sick, and they shall recover.

— Mark 16:17,18

It's important to note that in the original Greek text, it actually says, "And these signs shall follow them that *are believing*...." That means if you're not actively engaging your faith, you won't see these things happen. To see the visible manifestation of these signs following you, you have to be *believing* for them. People who cast out devils, speak with new tongues, and see the sick recover when they pray and lay hands on them are those who are releasing their faith and trusting God to do what He said He would do in His Word.

[For a deeper understanding of all these signs, including what it means to "take up serpents and drink any deadly thing and not be hurt," it is recommended that you obtain Rick Renner's series *"These Signs Shall Follow Them That Believe."*]

When we come to Mark 16:19, we read the first documentation of Jesus' ascension. It says, "So then after the Lord had spoken unto them, he was received up into heaven, and sat on the right hand of God." Verse 20, the very last verse of Mark's gospel, says, "And they went forth, and preached every where, the Lord working with them, and confirming the word with signs following. Amen."

Luke's Gospel Also Details Jesus' Departure

Next, we look at the sacred writings of the historian Luke who documented Jesus as saying, "And, behold, I send the promise of my Father upon you: but tarry ye in the city of Jerusalem, until ye be endued with power from on high" (Luke 24:49). The word "behold" here is the Greek word *idou*, which is a term expressing great *wonder* and *amazement*. It's Luke's way of injecting his — or Jesus'— excitement into the text. It is the equivalent of him saying, "Wow! What I'm about to tell you is so amazing that it nearly leaves me speechless. Listen to this!"

Jesus was absolutely thrilled beyond words that He was about to send the promised gift of the baptism in the Holy Spirit. It was — and is — the most magnificent gift we as believers can receive, next to our salvation.

But in order for the apostles to receive this gift, they needed to tarry in the city of Jerusalem until they were clothed with supernatural power from Heaven.

After giving His disciples these words of instruction, the Bible says, "And he [Jesus] led them out as far as to Bethany, and he lifted up his hands, and blessed them. And it came to pass, while he blessed them, he was parted from them, and carried up into heaven" (Luke 24:50,51). Here we find the second eyewitness account of Jesus' ascension into Heaven.

As the disciples watched Him rise into the sky out of their sight, "…They worshipped him, and returned to Jerusalem with great joy: And were continually in the temple, praising and blessing God. Amen" (Luke 24:52,53).

The Book of Acts Connects Jesus' Ascension With His Second Coming

History tells us that the book of Acts was also written by Luke sometime between 63 and 70 AD, and in his first chapter, he recounts and expands upon what took place the day Jesus ascended into Heaven. Luke wrote, "When they therefore were come together, they asked of him, saying, Lord, wilt thou at this time restore again the kingdom to Israel? And he said unto them, It is not for you to know the times or the seasons, which the Father hath put in his own power. But ye shall receive power, after that the Holy Ghost is come upon you: and ye shall be witnesses unto me both in Jerusalem, and in all Judaea, and in Samaria, and unto the uttermost part of the earth" (Acts 1:6-8).

Please note the word "power" in verse 8. It's the amazing Greek word *dunamis*, which describes *explosive power that produces unparalleled results*. In addition to being the source of the word *dynamite*, it is also the very word that was used to describe *the full force of an advancing army*. Moreover, it is the Greek term that was used to depict *the force of nature* like a tornado, an earthquake, or a hurricane.

Jesus' use of this word *dunamis* — translated here as "power" — is the equivalent of Him saying, "You're going to receive supernatural, explosive power from the Father that is going to strengthen you spiritually so that you become as powerful as an advancing army! In fact, you're going to receive such extraordinary strength that you'll be able to shake things up spiritually like an earthquake and blow things out of the way like a spiritual tornado or hurricane. When the power (*dunamis*) of the Holy Spirit has come upon you, you'll be witnesses for Me in Jerusalem, Judea, Samaria, and in the uttermost parts of the earth."

Luke then tells us, "And when he had spoken these things, while they beheld, he was taken up; and a cloud received him out of their sight. And while they looked stedfastly toward heaven as he went up, behold, two men stood by them in white apparel; which also said, Ye men of Galilee, why stand ye gazing up into heaven? this same Jesus, which is taken up from you into heaven, shall so come in like manner as ye have seen him go into heaven" (Acts 1:9-11).

Here in verse 11, we see the angels declare what the Second Coming of Christ will be like. Just as He was gradually taken up into Heaven, He will gradually descend from Heaven and return to the earth. This is a description of Zechariah's prophecy regarding the day of the Lord (*see* Zechariah 14:1-4). It, too, is a tenet of the Christian faith listed in The Apostles' Creed, which we'll cover in a coming lesson.

Jesus' 'Great Commission' Was Given the Day of His Ascension

There is another account of what Jesus said the day He returned to Heaven, and it is found in Matthew's gospel. Although the actual ascension is not mentioned, it does record the Great Commission Jesus gave to all His followers just before returning to Heaven. Matthew 28:16-20 says:

> Then the eleven disciples went away into Galilee, into a mountain where Jesus had appointed them.
>
> And when they saw him, they worshipped him: but some doubted.
>
> And Jesus came and spake unto them, saying, All power is given unto me in heaven and in earth.
>
> Go ye therefore, and teach all nations, baptizing them in the name of the Father, and of the Son, and of the Holy Ghost:
>
> Teaching them to observe all things whatsoever I have commanded you: and, lo, I am with you always, even unto the end of the world. Amen.

Notice Jesus' words in verse 19: "Go ye therefore." The original Greek text actually says, *"Go and keep on going."* This lets us know that Jesus is not telling us to simply take one or two mission trips in our lifetime. Instead, He is instructing us to make sharing the Gospel a way of life! Even if we cannot personally go — and keep on going — we can prayerfully partner with individuals and ministries who continue to go and teach all nations.

A Special Promise to All Who 'Go and Keep on Going'

Interestingly, Jesus made a promise to any believer, church, or ministry organization that will *go and keep on going* with the Gospel to reach those near and those who are abroad. He said, "…And, lo, I am with you always, even unto the end of the world. Amen" (Matthew 28:20). The word "lo" here is an exclamatory promise Jesus made to anyone who will, in any fashion, "go" and take the Gospel to the lost. In other words, the "lo" is for those who will "go."

In Greek, the use of the word "lo" is the equivalent of saying, "And, WOW, will I ever be with you — even to the ends of the earth!" Essentially, Jesus was saying, "If you will go and keep going — doing all you can in every way possible to preach and teach the Gospel — *WOW, I promise that you will experience My amazing presence in the doing of it!*"

Christ promises His powerful presence will be enjoyed and experienced by all believers who are totally committed to discovering their part by the direction of the Holy Spirit and then *going* to the lost with the message of salvation. This means if believers want to experience the power of God, they must act on what triggers its release. Jesus' promise is that His supernatural, powerful presence will accompany all who will do their part to take the good news of salvation to others!

Again, it's in the *going* that the power of the Holy Spirit is triggered, and its release is experienced. Whether you personally go and keep going or support others who go, Jesus said, *"And, WOW, will My presence and power ever be with you — even to the ends of the earth!"* With these words, Jesus blessed His disciples and ascended into Heaven, and one day in the very soon future, He will come again!

In our next lesson, we will search the Scriptures and learn about Jesus' current location and vocation — seated at the right hand of God the Father in Heaven, making intercession for us.

STUDY QUESTIONS

> Study to shew thyself approved unto God, a workman that needeth not to be ashamed, rightly dividing the word of truth.
> — 2 Timothy 2:15

1. Carefully read the account of Jesus' ascension into Heaven in Acts 1:9-12 along with the Old Testament description of His Second Coming in Zechariah 14:3,4 (*see* also Jude 14). In what ways are these two events *similar*? How is Christ's Second Coming different than His return to rapture the Church, which we read about in First Thessalonians 4:16,17 and 5:1-3?

2. Jesus, the Son of God, taught as much — if not more — about hell than any other topic. Look up these verses and identify some of the most important things He said about this horrific place during His ministry. Ask the Lord to let these sobering truths motivate you to be ready to share the Gospel whenever the opportunity arises! (*See* First Peter 3:15.)

   - Matthew 7:13,14
   - Mark 9:43-49 (also in Matthew 5:30; 18:8,9)
   - Matthew 24:45-51; 25:24-30
   - Luke 12;4,5
   - Matthew 25:41-46
   - Luke 16:19-31

3. Just before ascending into Heaven, Jesus urgently instructed His followers not to leave Jerusalem to do anything until they were first clothed with the power of the Holy Spirit (*see* Luke 24:49; Acts 1:4,5,8). Indeed, if the baptism in the Holy Spirit was so vital to Jesus' followers then, it is equally vital to us now. Have you received this indescribable gift? What did Jesus say in Luke 11:9-13 we are to do to receive the infilling of the Holy Spirit?

PRACTICAL APPLICATION

> But be ye doers of the word, and not hearers only, deceiving your own selves.
> — James 1:22

1. Jesus promises His powerful presence will accompany all who will do their part to take the good news of salvation to others! It's in the going that the power of the Holy Spirit is triggered and experienced in your life. In what ways are you sharing the Gospel with others? Are you supporting a ministry that is bringing the Good News to the lost? If so, what ministry, and how are you supporting them?
2. In Mark 16:17,18, Jesus mentions four specific supernatural signs that will follow those who believe in Him. Are you seeing these signs? Are you actively engaging your faith — believing that these things will happen in and through *you*? Pray and ask the Holy Spirit to help you begin to build your faith by feeding on the Word (Romans 10:17), praying in the Spirit (Jude 20), and recalling to mind all the wonderful things He's already done in your life (Psalm 77:11,12).

LESSON 9

TOPIC
He Sits at the Right Hand of God the Father Almighty

SCRIPTURES
1. **Ephesians 1:20,21** — Which he wrought in Christ, when he raised him from the dead, and set him at his own right hand in the heavenly places, far above all principality, and power, and might, and dominion, and every name that is named, not only in this world, but also in that which is to come.
2. **1 Peter 3:22** — Who is gone into heaven, and is on the right hand of God; angels and authorities and powers being made subject unto him.
3. **Hebrews 8:6** — But now hath obtained a more excellent ministry, by how much also he is the mediator of a better covenant, which was established upon better promises.
4. **Hebrews 7:24,25** — But this man, because he continueth ever, hath an unchangeable priesthood. Wherefore he is able also to save them to the uttermost that come unto God by him, seeing he ever liveth to make intercession for them.

5. **Hebrews 4:15,16** — For we have not an high priest which cannot be touched with the feeling of our infirmities; but was in all points tempted like as we are, yet without sin. Let us therefore come boldly unto the throne of grace, that we may obtain mercy, and find grace to help in time of need.

GREEK WORDS

1. "boldly" — παρρησία (*parresia*): freedom of speech; it presents the picture of a person who speaks his mind and who does it straightforwardly and with great confidence
2. "obtain" — λαμβάνω (*lambano*): to seize or to lay hold of something in order to make it your very own; it is the picture of reaching out to grab, to capture, or to take possession of something; depending on the context in which it is used, it can mean to violently lay hold of something, to seize and take it as one's very own, or it can depict a person who gently and graciously receives something that is freely and easily given
3. "find" — εὑρίσκω (*heurisko*): to find; a discovery made by searching; usually denotes a discovery made due to an intense investigation, scientific study, or scholarly research
4. "help" — βοήθεια (*boetheia*): a word with a military connotation; it can be translated to help meet someone's need, but first and foremost it was used to describe that moment when a soldier got into trouble; when his fellow soldiers were alerted to his dangerous situation, they were completely dedicated to the goal of going into battle to defend their co-fighter and fighting for his well-being, safety, and security; just hearing that a fellow soldier was in need was enough to beckon the other soldiers into battle and to motivate them to spare no effort in order to rescue him and bring him back to a place of safety and protection

SYNOPSIS

After Jesus' work on the Cross was finished and He was raised from the dead, He revealed Himself to His disciples and followers for 40 days. He then ascended into Heaven where He now sits at the right hand of God the Father. His priceless sacrifice completely paid for all our sins — past, present, and future. Now, He serves as our Great High Priest, praying for us and pleading our case before God. The fact that Jesus is seated at the right hand of the Father is mentioned throughout the New Testament and is another major tenet of the Christian faith enshrined in The Apostles' Creed.

The emphasis of this lesson:

After Jesus accomplished His work on the Cross and was raised from the dead, God the Father seated Him at His right hand in Heaven. He now serves as our Great High Priest, ever interceding in prayer on our behalf to God. The Holy Spirit invites us to fearlessly and confidently approach the Father any time and freely speak what is on our heart.

A Review of The Apostles' Creed and Its History

What is called The Apostles' Creed dates back to approximately 140 AD in its oldest form and was first known as The Old Roman Creed. The version we use today likely dates back to approximately 390 AD. It is a concentrated collection of the teachings of the apostles, and hence, the reason it is referred to as The Apostles' Creed. Early Church fathers referred to it as "the rule of faith," as it covers the irrefutable core beliefs of the Christian faith. In the centuries that followed, The Apostles' Creed was used as a "truth filter" to determine what was and wasn't genuine Christian doctrine, and it is still widely used today in denominations all over the world. Here again is The Apostles' Creed:

> **I believe in God, the Father Almighty,**
> **the Creator of heaven and earth,**
> **and in Jesus Christ, His only Son, our Lord:**
> **Who was conceived of the Holy Spirit,**
> **born of the Virgin Mary,**
> **suffered under Pontius Pilate,**
> **was crucified, died, and was buried.**
> **He descended into hell.**
> **The third day He arose again from the dead.**
> **He ascended into heaven**
> **and sits at the right hand of God the Father Almighty,**
> **whence He shall come to judge the living and the dead.**

> I believe in the Holy Spirit,
> the holy catholic [universal] church,
> the communion of saints,
> the forgiveness of sins,
> the resurrection of the body,
> and life everlasting. Amen.

'I Believe... [Jesus] Sits at the Right Hand of God the Father Almighty'

When something is repeated throughout Scripture, it indicates both its importance and its validity. Jesus' current location at the Father's right hand is one such repeated fact. Ephesians 1:20 and 21 tells us that "…[God] raised him [Jesus] from the dead, and set him at his own right hand in the heavenly places, far above all principality, and power, and might, and dominion, and every name that is named, not only in this world, but also in that which is to come." (For a detailed review of the meaning of this passage, please refer back to Lesson 6.)

In a similar way, First Peter 3:22 says, "[Jesus] is gone into heaven, and is on the right hand of God; angels and authorities and powers being made subject unto him." When we factor in the original Greek meaning in this passage, the *Renner Interpretive Version (RIV)* of First Peter 3:22 reads:

> **Who is at the authoritative right hand of God — having journeyed into the highest heavens, with angelic creatures, and those who hold public office and wield authority entrusted to them through election or by governmental decree, and all other known and unknown forces and powers in the universe being made subordinate, subjected, and submitted to Him and to His authority.**

Again and again, this truth is repeated throughout Scripture, including the books of Acts, Romans, Second Corinthians, Colossians, and Hebrews. The truth that Jesus sits at the right hand of the Father is unquestionably one of the most important beliefs of the Christian faith as it points to Jesus' present-day ministry to all believers.

Jesus Now Serves As Our Great High Priest

When Jesus' feet lifted from the earth, He was received into Heaven, and Hebrews 8:6 tells us that He started the next phase of His ministry. A phase so wonderful that the writer calls it "…a more excellent ministry, by how much also he is the mediator of a better covenant, which was established upon better promises."

The Greek word for "excellent" here means *incomparable*, *unparalleled*, *unsurpassed*, *unmatched*, *finest*, *greatest*, or *most excellent*. This means Jesus' present-day ministry is not even to be compared to His previous earthly ministry. It is unparalleled, unsurpassed, and extraordinary. Indeed, Hebrews 8:6 emphatically lets us know that Jesus' current ministry is His finest, greatest, and most excellent ministry.

Why is this phase of Jesus' ministry so excellent? What is He doing right now that is so mighty? The moment Jesus sat down at the Father's right hand, His ministry was initiated as the Great High Priest to everyone who calls on His name. Under the Old Covenant, there were *many* priests, but each of them eventually died due to their human condition.

Hebrews 7:24 and 25 declares, "But this man [Jesus], because he continueth ever, hath an unchangeable priesthood. Wherefore he is able also to save them to the uttermost that come unto God by him, seeing that he ever liveth to make intercession for them." Jesus, our Great High Priest, lived a sinless life, and He now serves as our eternal prayer warrior in Heaven!

The writer of Hebrews describes Jesus' present-day ministry saying, "For we have not an high priest which cannot be touched with the feeling of our infirmities; but was in all points tempted like as we are, yet without sin" (Hebrews 4:15). This verse makes it clear that Jesus understands every problem and every temptation that you have or that you'll ever face. Why? Because He was fully man when He walked the earth and is personally acquainted with and understands every single temptation that human beings experience. But Jesus faced them and didn't sin! For that reason, He is qualified to sit at the Father's right hand and to intercede on your behalf.

How Are We To Respond and Cooperate With Jesus' Work As Our Great High Priest?

Come 'Boldly' Into God's Presence

Hebrews 4:16 says, "Let us therefore come boldly unto the throne of grace, that we may obtain mercy, and find grace to help in time of need." The word "boldly" in this verse is the Greek word *parresia*, which describes *freedom of speech*. It presents the picture of *a person who speaks his mind* and who does it *straightforwardly and with great confidence*.

In New Testament times, the word *parresia* depicted a *frankness* that was so bold, it was regularly met with resistance, hostility, and opposition. It just wasn't acceptable to speak so candidly. When someone spoke his mind and his thoughts this freely, his outspokenness was met with rebuke. In this case, the Holy Spirit uses the word *parresia* to urge us to come "boldly" before the throne of grace and invites us to be straight-to-the-point when we talk to Jesus!

Friend, you need never fear that you are too frank, too bold, too forthright, too honest, too outspoken, or too blunt when you open your heart to God about your needs and struggles or when you request His help. Of course, you should never be irreverent, but neither do you need to be afraid to speak exactly what is on your heart. The Greek word *parresia* emphatically tells you that Jesus will never be turned off, offended, or insulted when you freely speak your heart and mind to Him. He wants to hear what you have to say!

'Obtain' His Mercy

As you unashamedly approach God in prayer, He wants you to "obtain mercy" (Hebrews 4:16). The Greek word translated as "obtain" here is a form of the word *lambano*, which means *to seize or to lay hold of something in order to make it your very own*. It is the picture of reaching out to grab, to capture, or to take possession of something. Depending on the context in which it is used, the word *lambano* can mean *to violently lay hold of something to seize and take it as one's very own*, or it can depict *a person who gently and graciously receives something that is freely and easily given*.

The reality is there will be moments in your life when you can easily reach out by faith and graciously receive the mercy Jesus is offering. There will also be hard moments where the struggle is so intense that you'll have to reach out and forcibly lay hold of the help God offers you. In both cases, Jesus is ready and willing to simply give you what you need — no questions asked. All you have to do is open your heart and, by faith, receive it.

So if you're feeling overwhelmed, shove those negative circumstances and emotions out of the way and reach out by faith to lay hold of the grace and mercy that Jesus freely offers. It's time for you to receive what He wants to give to you.

'Find' His Grace

When you're in God's presence grabbing hold of His mercy, He also wants you to "find grace" (Hebrews 4:16). The word "find" in this passage is a form of the Greek word *heurisko*, which means *to find*, and it describes *a discovery made by searching*. It usually denotes *a discovery made due to an intense investigation, scientific study, or scholarly research*. After working long hours and searching, the researcher suddenly finds what he has been seeking. In that unforgettable moment of joyful euphoria, he shrieks, "EUREKA! I FOUND IT!"

The use of this word *heurisko* tells us that God's help doesn't usually come by happenstance. Yet, if we will investigate, study, and diligently search for His help, we, too, will come to that *eureka* moment when we "find" the help we need to overcome what we're facing in life. Once you seize the answer from Heaven, such euphoria will flood your heart that you will exclaim, "I HAVE IT!" "I'VE FOUND IT!" or "I'VE RECEIVED IT!"

Essentially, Hebrews 4:16 means you can go to Jesus — our Great High Priest — to obtain mercy and find help for yourself and for others about whom you are worried or burdened. This is good news…

- For those who need healing for their bodies.
- For those who are bound and need deliverance.
- For those who are tormented and need peace.
- For marriages and families that are in trouble.
- For provision to be given to those who need a financial breakthrough.
- For those who are in need in any area of their lives.

Not only can you take your own needs to Jesus, but you can also take the needs of others to Him and obtain the help they so desperately need.

Receive God's Help in Your Time of Need

Along with obtaining mercy and finding grace, Jesus offers "help in time of need" (Hebrews 4:16). The word "help" here is the Greek word *boetheia*, a word with a military connotation. Although it can be translated as meaning to help meet someone else's need, first and foremost the word *boetheia* was used to describe *the moment when a soldier got into trouble and his fellow soldiers were alerted to his dangerous situation.* Immediately, they were completely dedicated to the goal of going into battle to defend their co-fighter — fighting for his well-being, safety, and security. Just hearing that a fellow soldier was in need was enough to beckon the other soldiers into battle and motivate them to spare no effort in order to rescue him and bring him back to a place of safety and protection.

The fact that the word *boetheia* (help) is used in this text lets us know that when we get into trouble and Jesus hears about it, He will come to our defense! He will do battle for us in our time of need. If we will go to Jesus — our Great High Priest — and present our case to Him, He will rise up like a Mighty Warrior who is ready to go into battle to fight for us until we are delivered and free.

Think about it: Why would we ever try to fight our battles alone when the Greatest Warrior in the universe — the One who possesses ultimate power — wants to fight for us? This is the best news ever! Jesus has become our Great High Priest! He is *your* personal Representative who sits at the right hand of the Father in Heaven, making intercession for you and anyone who comes to Him by faith. From His highly exalted place, He has His eyes fixed on you, and at this very moment, He is fighting for you and every believer who seeks His assistance. Praise His mighty Name!

In Lesson 10, we will peer into the future and focus on the statement of faith that Christ shall come to judge the living and the dead.

STUDY QUESTIONS

Study to shew thyself approved unto God, a workman that needeth not to be ashamed, rightly dividing the word of truth.
— 2 Timothy 2:15

1. There is absolutely no one like Jesus! There are certain things that only He can do, and you need to be aware of them. According to these verses, what works are exclusive to Christ?
   - Acts 4:12
   - 1 Timothy 2:5
   - Matthew 3:11 and Luke 3:16
2. To help you get a well-rounded view of Jesus' new role at the right hand of the Father in Heaven, take a few moments to look up these passages and note the details that are unique in each verse. How do these truths expand your understanding of Jesus' work on your behalf?
   - Luke 22:69
   - Acts 2:30-36
   - Acts 5:30,31
   - Romans 8:33,34
   - Colossians 3:1-3
   - Hebrews 1:8,9
   - Hebrews 10:11-14
   - Hebrews 12:1,2
3. The book of Hebrews has much to say about Jesus' role as our Great High Priest. As you spend time in the Word of God this week, read through Hebrews 7, 8, 9, and 10, which note how Jesus' ministry is different — and far superior — to the ministry of every other priest on earth. How do these chapters help you have a greater appreciation for Jesus as your Great High Priest?

PRACTICAL APPLICATION

> But be ye doers of the word, and not hearers only, deceiving your own selves.
> —James 1:22

1. God instructs us to "boldly" approach His throne in prayer, which means He invites us to be *confident*, *forthright*, and *straight to the point* with whatever is on our heart. Do you feel this level of freedom when you come to the Father in prayer? Or do you fear He will be offended,

angry, or be turned off if you freely speak your mind? If you struggle at times to pour out your heart to Him, ask the Holy Spirit to show you the root cause and remove it from you by His mighty power.

2. Hebrews 4:16 tells us that God provides us with timely "help" — the Greek word *boetheia* — which means when you're in trouble and Jesus hears about it, He will come to your defense! Take time to meditate on this powerful passage in Hebrews 2:14,15,17 and 18 in the *Amplified Classic Version*.

Since, therefore, [these His] children share in flesh and blood [in the physical nature of human beings], He [Himself] in a similar manner partook of the same [nature], that by [going through] death He might bring to nought and make of no effect him who had the power of death — that is, the devil — And also that He might deliver and completely set free all those who through the [haunting] fear of death were held in bondage throughout the whole course of their lives.

So it is evident that it was essential that He be made like His brethren in every respect, in order that He might become a merciful (sympathetic) and faithful High Priest in the things related to God, to make atonement and propitiation for the people's sins. For because He Himself [in His humanity] has suffered in being tempted (tested and tried), He is able [immediately] to run to the cry of (assist, relieve) those who are being tempted and tested and tried [and who therefore are being exposed to suffering].

What is the Holy Spirit speaking to you through these verses?

LESSON 10

TOPIC

He Shall Come To Judge the Living and the Dead

SCRIPTURES

1. **2 Timothy 4:1** — I charge thee therefore before God, and the Lord Jesus Christ, who shall judge the quick and the dead at his appearing and his kingdom.
2. **1 Peter 4:5** — Who shall give account to him that is ready to judge the quick and the dead.
3. **Jude 14,15** — And Enoch also, the seventh from Adam, prophesied of these, saying, Behold, the Lord cometh with ten thousands of his saints, to execute judgment upon all, and to convince all that are ungodly....
4. **Romans 14:12** — So then every one of us shall give account of himself to God.
5. **2 Corinthians 5:10** — For we must all appear before the judgment seat of Christ; that every one may receive the things done in his body, according to that he hath done, whether it be good or bad.
6. **Revelation 20:12-15** — And I saw the dead, small and great, stand before God; and the books were opened: and another book was opened, which is the book of life: and the dead were judged out of those things which were written in the books, according to their works. And the sea gave up the dead which were in it; and death and hell delivered up the dead which were in them: and they were judged every man according to their works. And death and hell were cast into the lake of fire. This is the second death. And whosoever was not found written in the book of life was cast into the lake of fire.

GREEK WORDS

1. "judge" — κρίνω (*krino*): a word that usually referred to a jury who had just handed down their final sentence in a court of law; pictures

a verdict or a final sentence that is pronounced as the result of a court trial
2. "quick" — ζῶντας (*zontas*): describes those who are living
3. "dead" — νεκρος (*nekros*): the dead, or a life permanently terminated, hence, a lifeless corpse, a cadaver with no life left in it, or a body disconnected from life
4. "shall give" — ἀποδίδωμι (*apodidomi*): used here in a legal sense to denote one who gives an answer in a court of law
5. "account" — λόγον (*logon*): used in a legal sense to depict a legal account or a legal reckoning
6. "ready" — ἑτοίμως (*hetoimos*): the actions of one who has done his part to be prepared for a specific event; also used in an athletic sense to depict runners who had prepared in advance for a race and who were ready and raring to go; in a military sense, this word also portrayed soldiers who had their shoes tied on very tightly, hence, they had a firm footing and were ready for action
7. "execute judgment" — κρίσις (*krisis*): a decision made by a legal court, a court decree, a legal procedure at the court, or a verdict delivered that results in judgment
8. "upon" — κατά (*kata*): a preposition that means against and carries the idea of a strike against them so strong that it is inescapable
9. "all" — πάντας (*pantas*): all-inclusive, and here it means everyone with no exceptions
10. "convince" — ἐλέγχω (*elegcho*): a legal term meaning to expose, to convict, or to cross-examine for the purpose of conviction, as when convicting a lawbreaker in a court of law; pictures a lawyer who brings forth evidence that is indisputable and undeniable; it means in that day Heaven's court will present all the proof necessary to irrefutably back up a charge of guilt against the ungodly

SYNOPSIS

Judgment day — a future event that both Christians and many non-Christians believe in. In fact, it is a prolific premise in some of Hollywood's top-grossing films of all time. Although some believe it to be merely money-making fiction, the truth is every person — from every generation that has ever lived — will one day stand before Almighty God and give an account of his or her life. This is another primary teaching of

Jesus and the original apostles — and an integral part of The Apostles' Creed.

The emphasis of this lesson:

A time is coming when every person who has ever lived will one day stand before God and give an account for what they've said and done in this life. The ungodly will be tried by God at the White Throne Judgment, and believers' lives will be evaluated at the Judgment Seat of Christ. The Lord is fully prepared to execute a fair and final judgment for all.

A Review of The Apostles' Creed and Its History

The Apostles' Creed, which dates back to approximately 140 AD in its oldest form, was first known as The Old Roman Creed. During its development in the Second Century, there was a great amount of false doctrine running rampant in the Church. To deal with this dilemma, Church leaders came together to forge a written, concentrated collection of the teachings of the apostles — hence, the reason it is called The Apostles' Creed.

Early Church fathers referred to it as "the rule of faith," as it covers the undeniable core beliefs of the Christian faith. In the centuries that followed, The Apostles' Creed was used as a "truth filter" to determine what was and wasn't genuine Christian doctrine. If there was ever a time we needed to know and understand this valuable creed, it's now! In these last of the last days, the Bible says a notable number of people will depart from the Christian faith and begin listening to and believing seducing spirits and doctrines of demons (*see* 1 Timothy 4:1). To help us remain anchored in the truth and avoid becoming a statistic of those who fall away, we are studying and committing to memory The Apostles' Creed:

I believe in God, the Father Almighty,
the Creator of heaven and earth,
and in Jesus Christ, His only Son, our Lord:
Who was conceived of the Holy Spirit,
born of the Virgin Mary,
suffered under Pontius Pilate,

was crucified, died, and was buried.
He descended into hell.
The third day He arose again from the dead.
He ascended into heaven
and sits at the right hand of God the Father Almighty,
whence He shall come to judge the living and the dead.
I believe in the Holy Spirit,
the holy catholic [universal] church,
the communion of saints,
the forgiveness of sins,
the resurrection of the body,
and life everlasting. Amen.

Paul Wrote About the Coming Judgment in His Letter to Timothy

In his very last letter, the apostle Paul wrote to his spiritual son, Timothy, and said, "I charge thee therefore before God, and the Lord Jesus Christ, who shall judge the quick and the dead at his appearing and his kingdom; Preach the word; be instant in season, out of season; reprove, rebuke, exhort with all long suffering and doctrine" (2 Timothy 4:1,2).

The belief that Jesus will one day judge all of mankind was — and still is — a powerful motivating force to share the Gospel with others. In verse 1, Paul said that Jesus will "judge the quick and the dead." The word "judge" here in Greek is *krino*, which is a word that usually referred to *a jury who had just handed down their final sentence in a court of law*. It pictures a verdict or a final sentence that is pronounced as the result of a court trial.

By using this word *krino* — translated here as "judge" — we understand that when Jesus comes, the court of Heaven will have already examined all the evidence, and it will hand down a verdict to the "quick and the dead." The word "quick" is the Greek word *zontas*, which emphatically describes *those who are living* at the time of Christ's appearing. In contrast, the word "dead" is *nekros*, the Greek word for *dead*, or *a life permanently terminated*. Hence, this is *a lifeless corpse, a cadaver with no life left in it*, or *a body disconnected from life*.

Second Timothy 4:1 clearly states that there is coming a day when Jesus Himself will hand down the final verdict to every man and woman who has ever lived. Not only will He judge those who are alive at the time of His return, but He will also resurrect those who died and pass judgment on them.

Jesus Is 'Ready To Judge the Quick and the Dead'

This sobering truth is echoed almost word for word in First Peter 4:5, which states, "Who shall give account to him that is ready to judge the quick and the dead." Notice the phrase "shall give." It is a translation of the Greek word *apodidomi*, which is a compound of the words *apo* and *didomi*. The word *apo* means *to return* or refers to *something that moves back*, and the word *didomi* means *to give*. When we join these two words to form *apodidomi*, it means *to give back*, *to report*, or *to give an accounting*. In this verse, it is used in a legal sense to denote *one who gives an answer in a court of law*.

Under the inspiration of the Holy Spirit, Peter reminds us there is coming a time in the future when every person who has ever lived will one day take the witness stand and give an account for what he or she has said and done in this life. The word "account" here is the Greek term *logon*, and in a legal sense, it depicts *a legal account* or *a legal reckoning*. Indeed, absolutely nothing escapes "…the eyes of Him with whom we have to do" (Hebrews 4:13).

The Bible says Jesus is "…ready to judge the quick and the dead" (1 Peter 4:5). The word "ready" in this passage is very important. It is the Greek word *hetoimos*, and it describes *the actions of one who has done his part to be prepared for a specific event*. It was also used in an athletic sense to depict *runners who had prepared in advance for a race and who were ready and raring to go*. In a military sense, this word also portrayed *soldiers who had their shoes tied on very tightly*. Hence, they had a firm footing and were ready for action.

The use of the word *hetoimos* — translated here as "ready" — tells us God is ready for the Day of Judgment. He has done His homework and is totally prepared, having done everything necessary to be ready for the judgment that is about to occur. The court of Heaven has a firm footing regarding all the evidence and details it has observed and knows to be factually true.

When that moment of judgment finally comes, the Judge of Heaven will be fully informed and will be ready and raring to issue a verdict of judgment against the deeds of the ungodly that will be based on the solid evidence that Heaven has observed.

The Ungodly Will Not Escape God's Judgment

Interestingly, the word "judge" in First Peter 4:5 is the word *krino* — the same word used by Paul in Second Timothy 4:1 — which usually referred to *a jury who had just handed down their final sentence in a court of law*. Again, it pictures *a verdict or a final sentence that is pronounced as the result of a court trial*.

This lets us know that after all the evidence has been presented and the Judge of Heaven has examined all the facts, a final verdict will be issued by the court of Heaven. This verse should be very troubling to the ungodly who don't know God and who try to convince themselves that they will somehow bypass or escape divine judgment, for this verse clearly states that a day of judgment will come to all the ungodly at a moment in the future.

To be clear, this verse is *not* referring to the Judgment Seat of Christ, which will be a place where rewards are given to faithful believers. It refers to the Great White Throne judgment at which moment all the ungodly will be summoned before the court of Heaven. The word "quick" is again the Greek word *zontas*, and here it refers to the ungodly who are *living*. These words should be taken as a warning that there are times when God's judgment falls upon the wicked even while they are living.

A careful study of both the Old and New Testaments reveals vivid examples of the judgment of God falling upon the wicked while they were living. Nevertheless, when Jesus comes, He will judge both those who are alive and those who are dead. In Greek, the word for "dead" here is *nekros*, which describes *the dead* or *a life permanently terminated*. Hence, it is *a lifeless corpse, a cadaver with no life left in it*, or *a body disconnected from life*.

Now, God is not in the business of judging human corpses, so this emphatically means He will judge those who once lived in those now-dead bodies. The ungodly "dead" (*nekros*) will be resurrected to stand trial before God. This is a divine warning to all ungodly that they will ultimately be judged, regardless of whether they are alive or dead. Death itself will not enable them to circumvent this future judgment.

Taking into account the original Greek meaning in this verse, here is the *Renner Interpretive Version (RIV)* of First Peter 4:5:

> **Those who do this to you will eventually be required to give a full account and legal reckoning to God, who is fully informed about their actions, and when that moment comes, He will be prepared and ready to issue a verdict of judgment for those who are living and for those who are dead.**

Jude's Description of the Day of the Lord

Even Jude, the half-brother of Jesus, mentions the coming day of the Lord's judgment in his brief but powerful epistle. He said, "And Enoch also, the seventh from Adam, prophesied of these, saying, Behold, the Lord cometh with ten thousands of his saints, to execute judgment upon all, and to convince all that are ungodly…" (Jude 14,15).

Notice the phrase "execute judgment." It is a translation of the Greek word *krisis*, which is where we get the word *crisis*. It describes *a decision made by a legal court, a court decree, a legal procedure at the court*, or *a verdict delivered that results in judgment*. Jude says the Lord is coming to deliver His final verdict of judgment "upon all."

In Greek, the word "upon" is *kata*, a preposition that means *against* and carries the idea of *a strike against someone that is so strong it is inescapable*. The word "all" is the Greek word *pantas*, which is *all-inclusive*, and here it means *everyone with no exceptions*. Thus, Jesus is coming to deliver the final decision of Heaven's court against everyone without exception.

Interestingly, Jude quotes the Old Testament prophet Enoch who said the Lord is coming "…to convince all that are ungodly…" (Jude 15). The word "convince" is the Greek legal term *elegcho*, meaning *to expose, to convict*, or *to cross-examine for the purpose of conviction, as when convicting a lawbreaker in a court of law*. It pictures a lawyer who brings forth evidence that is indisputable and undeniable. The use of this word *elegcho* (convince) means in that day, Heaven's court will present all the proof necessary to irrefutably back up a charge of guilt against all the ungodly.

Taking into account the original Greek meaning in this verse, here is the *Renner Interpretive Version (RIV)* of Jude 15:

> **When He comes, He will carry out the irreversible charge that Heaven's court has issued inescapably against all so-charged.**

In the very same way a lawyer brings forth indisputable and undeniable evidence in a court of law, Heaven's court will present irrefutable and uncontestable evidence to prove a charge of guilt against the godless....

The Judgment Seat of Christ

We who know the Lord will not take part in God's judgment of the ungodly. Instead, we will each stand before the Judgment Seat of Christ, and while we will not be judged for our sin because it is covered by the Blood, we will be rewarded for what we did in the body. Romans 14:12 says, "So then every one of us shall give account of himself to God." Paul expands on this truth in Second Corinthians 5:10, where he says, "For we must all appear before the judgment seat of Christ; that every one may receive the things done in his body, according to that he hath done, whether it be good or bad."

Christ's evaluation of our obedience and corresponding works will take place *before* the final, Great White Throne judgment of the ungodly. Revelation 20:12-15 tells us what will happen to those who reject God and live as they please. Under the direction of the Holy Spirit, John wrote, "And I saw the dead, small and great, stand before God; and the books were opened: and another book was opened, which is the book of life: and the dead were judged out of those things which were written in the books, according to their works. And the sea gave up the dead which were in it; and death and hell delivered up the dead which were in them: and they were judged every man according to their works. And death and hell were cast into the lake of fire. This is the second death. And whosoever was not found written in the book of life was cast into the lake of fire."

Friend, the day of judgment for the ungodly is most assuredly coming. No one will escape it. Likewise, we who are in Christ will also be evaluated by Jesus at His judgment seat and rewarded accordingly for what we did for Him in this life. This is one of the foundational tenets of the Christian faith that is recorded in The Apostles' Creed.

In our next lesson, we will examine the foundational belief in the Holy Spirit.

STUDY QUESTIONS

> Study to shew thyself approved unto God, a workman that
> needeth not to be ashamed, rightly dividing the word of truth.
> — 2 Timothy 2:15

1. One thing is very clear about God's judgment — He is fair and accurate in His assessment of each person. How will He determine who deserves what? Review Psalm 62:12; Jeremiah 17:10; 32:19; Matthew 16:17; First Peter 1:17; and Revelation 22:12. What is the recurring theme in all these verses?
2. As a believer, each of us will stand before the Judgment Seat of Christ, and while we will not be judged for our sin because it is covered by the Blood, we will be evaluated for what we did during our life on earth. When you consider the prevailing truth from the scriptures in Study Question 1, along with the details presented by the apostle Paul in Second Corinthians 5:9,10 and First Corinthians 3:13-15, what will the Judgment Seat of Christ be like?
3. From Genesis to Revelation, God makes it clear that a day of reckoning is coming for the ungodly — a day when their lives will be carefully examined and a final verdict judgment pronounced. The Bible calls it the Great White Throne Judgment. Take a few moments to reflect on Revelation 20:11-15 and Matthew 25:31-46, and in your own words, describe what is going to take place. Who are you motivated to pray for and reach out to with the message of the Gospel so that they can avoid eternal separation from God?

PRACTICAL APPLICATION

> But be ye doers of the word, and not hearers only,
> deceiving your own selves.
> — James 1:22

1. How does knowing and being reminded that you will one day stand before God and give an account for your life affect the way you live? If you knew you only had one month to live and then stand before God, how would you live differently? What would you *stop* doing? What would you *start* doing?
2. It is interesting to note that in addition to the Book of Life, the Bible talks about other books in Heaven by which our lives will be judged

(*see* Revelation 20:12,13). According to Psalm 139:1-4, 13-16, and Malachi 3:16-18, what are two of these books that Christ will use to evaluate your life? How do these passages motivate you to live your life?

3. If the Holy Spirit is putting His finger on certain attitudes or actions in your life that are displeasing Him, take time now to make things right (*see* 1 John 1:9; Ezekiel 18:30-32; Acts 3:19). Repent of any wrong that you've done and ask God to cleanse you with the blood of Jesus and give you His grace to live holy and pleasing to Him.

LESSON 11

TOPIC
I Believe in the Holy Spirit

SCRIPTURES

1. **Genesis 1:1,2** — In the beginning God created the heaven and the earth. And the earth was without form, and void; and darkness was upon the face of the deep. And the Spirit of God moved upon the face of the waters.
2. **Acts 19:2** — …Have ye received the Holy Ghost since ye believed?… We have not so much as heard whether there be any Holy Ghost.
3. **Acts 19:6** — And when Paul had laid his hands upon them, the Holy Ghost came on them; and they spake with tongues, and prophesied.
4. **John 20:21,22** — Then said Jesus to them again, Peace be unto you: as my Father hath sent me, even so send I you. And when he had said this, he breathed on them, and saith unto them, Receive ye the Holy Ghost.
5. **Genesis 2:7** — And the Lord God formed man of the dust of the ground, and breathed into his nostrils the breath of life; and man became a living soul.
6. **Ephesians 1:13** — …After that ye heard the word of truth, the gospel of your salvation: in whom also after that ye believed, ye were sealed with that holy Spirit of promise.
7. **1 Corinthians 6:19** — …Your body is the temple of the Holy Ghost.…

8. **Luke 24:49** — And, behold, I send the promise of my Father upon you: but tarry ye in the city of Jerusalem, until ye be endued with power from on high.

GREEK WORDS
1. "breathed" — ἐμφυσάω (*emphusao*): to breathe into or to inflate
2. "receive" — Λάβετε (*labete*): to take right now or to actively receive
3. "sealed" — σφραγίζω (*sphragidzo*): a seal placed on a package after it had been examined and inspected to make sure it was fully intact and complete (the seal was proof that the product was flawless)
4. "temple" — ναός (*naos*): a highly decorated shrine or the inner sanctum where a god lived
5. "endued" — ἐνδύω (*enduo*): to be empowered; to sink comfortably into a set of clothes
6. "power" — δύναμις (*dunamis*): explosive, superhuman power with enormous energy that produces phenomenal, extraordinary, and unparalleled results; the force of an entire army; a force of nature, like a hurricane, tornado, or earthquake

SYNOPSIS
Another foundational belief of the Christian faith found in The Apostles' Creed is belief in the Holy Spirit. What's interesting is that the Holy Spirit is the first member of the Trinity to be mentioned in Scripture, and we see this in the very second verse! The Bible opens by saying, "In the beginning God created the heaven and the earth" (Genesis 1:1). In the next verse, we read:

> **And the earth was without form, and void; and darkness was upon the face of the deep. And *the Spirit of God* moved upon the face of the waters.**
> — **Genesis 1:2**

From the beginning of creation, we see a powerful precedent was set: when the Spirit of God is present, He brings divine movement! This pattern continues all the way through to the book of Revelation. And when the Holy Spirit moves, creative power is released. It is this divine movement and release of supernatural power that God wants to see happening in your life too!

The emphasis of this lesson:

The Holy Spirit is the dynamic source of power residing in every believer. His first work of grace in our life is salvation. Once we're born again into God's family, the second work of grace in our life is the baptism of the Holy Spirit. This supernatural empowerment of the Spirit is vital to live a victorious Christian life.

A Review of The Apostles' Creed

The Apostles' Creed dates back to about 140 AD in its oldest form and was earlier known as The Old Roman Creed. Early Church fathers called it "the rule of faith," as it covers the irrefutable core beliefs of the Christian faith. In the centuries that followed, The Apostles' Creed became a "truth filter" to determine what was and wasn't genuine Christian doctrine. It is still quoted by Christians today in churches across the globe. To help you commit these nonnegotiable truths to memory, here again is The Apostles' Creed:

> **I believe in God, the Father Almighty,**
> **the Creator of heaven and earth,**
> **and in Jesus Christ, His only Son, our Lord:**
> **Who was conceived of the Holy Spirit,**
> **born of the Virgin Mary,**
> **suffered under Pontius Pilate,**
> **was crucified, died, and was buried.**
> **He descended into hell.**
> **The third day He arose again from the dead.**
> **He ascended into heaven**
> **and sits at the right hand of God the Father Almighty,**
> **whence He shall come to judge the living and the dead.**
> **I believe in the Holy Spirit,**
> **the holy catholic [universal] church,**
> **the communion of saints,**
> **the forgiveness of sins,**
> **the resurrection of the body,**
> **and life everlasting. Amen.**

'I Believe in the Holy Spirit'

'HAVE YOU RECEIVED THE HOLY SPIRIT?'

In Acts 19, we see the apostle Paul returning to the city of Ephesus, and on this occasion, it is likely he took the inland road and entered the city through the Magnesia Gate. As he walked on the South Road, he met a group of disciples of John the Baptist, and he initiated his conversation by saying, "…Have ye received the Holy Ghost since ye believed? And they said unto him, We have not so much as heard whether there be any Holy Ghost" (Acts 19:2).

These disciples had been to Israel and heard the preaching of John the Baptist — that the Messiah was coming. Although they had repented of their sins and were baptized by John, they were not aware the Messiah had already come. So Paul shared the Gospel with them — informing them that the Messiah had indeed come, and His name was Jesus.

The Bible says, "When they heard this, they were baptized in the name of the Lord Jesus. And when Paul had laid his hands upon them, the Holy Ghost came on them; and they spake with tongues, and prophesied" (Acts 19:5,6). In these verses, we see two distinct works of grace: the salvation of these men and their baptism in the Holy Spirit.

God's *saving grace* provides forgiveness of sins and eternal life with Him in Heaven. Once these disciples were saved, Paul knew they needed to be baptized in the Holy Spirit. It is this second work of grace that provides the needed power for living a victorious life. The same is true of believers today — including you. To effectively live the Christian life, it is vital we be filled with the Holy Spirit.

Salvation Is the *First* Work of Grace

The first amazing work of God's grace in a person's life is salvation, and we see this saving grace in action for the first time in John's gospel. Just after Jesus' resurrection from the dead, He appeared to the disciples who were in the upper room, hiding behind closed doors. After showing them His hands and side and convincing them it was Him, Jesus said, "Peace be unto you: as my Father hath sent me, even so send I you. And when he had said this, he breathed on them, and saith unto them, Receive ye the Holy Ghost" (John 20:21,22). It was in this moment the disciples were born again under the New Covenant in Christ. This is the first time in human history that salvation occurred among mankind.

In the Old Testament times, the Spirit of God came upon people temporarily for a certain task. Once the task was completed, the Holy Spirit would lift off the person and leave. The event recorded in John 20:22 is the first time the Spirit of God entered into people's hearts *permanently*. This was a distinct, separate experience that preceded the baptism in the Spirit they received on the day of Pentecost.

John 20:22 says Jesus "breathed on them." The word "breathed" is the Greek word *emphusao*, and it means *to breathe into* or *to inflate*. Just as a person breathes into a balloon, inflates the balloon, and the balloon now contains or holds this person's breath, Jesus Christ breathed His Spirit into their spirits, and in that moment, the disciples were born again.

Interestingly, the word for "breathed" here is the same one used in the Old Testament Septuagint in Genesis 2:7, where it says, "And the Lord God formed man of the dust of the ground, and *breathed into* his nostrils the breath of life; and man became a living soul." The phrase "breathed into" means God literally breathed into Adam, and Adam received the breath of God, which caused him to come alive. In the case of the apostles, Jesus breathed into them, and they received the Holy Spirit, causing them to come alive spiritually.

After Jesus breathed on the disciples, He said, "…Receive ye the Holy Ghost" (John 20:22). The word "receive" here is the Greek word *labete*, which is a direct form of the word *lambano*, and it means *to take right now* or *to actively receive*. The use of *labete* signifies that Jesus was not prophesying and telling His disciples about what was going to happen later. On the contrary, He was urging them to receive His Spirit *in that very moment*. And that was the moment His disciples were born again.

When the Holy Spirit entered their hearts and they were born again, peace flooded their souls. Remember, Jesus said to them, "Peace be unto you," the moment they were saved. Indeed, peace is the primary fruit of salvation. Everyone who repents of their sin and calls on the name of the Lord to be saved receives the Holy Spirit and has peace with God.

When You Are Saved, You Are Also Sealed With the Spirit

The apostle Paul wrote about our salvation in his letter to the believers in Ephesus: "…After that ye heard the word of truth, the gospel of your salvation: in whom also after that ye believed, ye were sealed with that holy Spirit of promise" (Ephesians 1:13). The word "sealed" is the Greek word *sphragidzo*, and it describes *a seal placed on a package after it had been examined and inspected to make sure it was fully intact and complete* (the seal was proof that the product was flawless). This seal also guaranteed a package would make it to its final destination and be treated with utmost care.

Once the Holy Spirit enters our spirit and the blood of Jesus has cleansed us, we are born again and made flawless in God's eyes! His seal is placed on us, guaranteeing we have been fully checked out and are complete in Him.

Taking into account the Greek meaning of this verse, here is the *RIV* (*Renner Interpretive Version*) of Ephesians 1:13:

> **When you were placed in Christ, God stamped you with a special seal and embossed it so deeply that it cannot be broken, erased, rubbed out, wiped out, deleted, or removed; that unbreakable seal is the Holy Spirit. Once you were stamped with Him, it meant you had God's approval. He examined the contents of your heart and found nothing flawed or inferior. And because everything was in order, He stamped you with the Holy Spirit, which is His seal of approval. Anyone who has this stamp is headed for special treatment. This seal means you belong to God and no one is to interfere with you as a "package."**
>
> **This "Holy Spirit stamp" means the postage is prepaid to get you all the way to your ultimate destination. That means you can be sure that once your journey with the Lord begins, you are going to make it all the way to where God wants you to go!**

First Corinthians 6:19 says that once you are saved, "…your body is the temple of the Holy Ghost." The word "temple" is the Greek word *naos*, and it describes *a highly decorated shrine or the inner sanctum where a god lived*. Thus, when you accepted Christ, the Holy Spirit moved inside you permanently, and you became a walking, talking cathedral of God. This is the first work of God's grace.

The Baptism of the Holy Spirit Is the *Second* Work of Grace

After the disciples were born again and just before Jesus ascended into Heaven, He said to His disciples, "And, behold, I send the promise of my Father upon you: but tarry ye in the city of Jerusalem, until ye be endued with power from on high" (Luke 24:49). Up until that point, the disciples had been saved and sealed with the Holy Spirit. They had become the "temple" of God, and His Spirit was living inside them. Had they died at that moment, they would have gone to Heaven. But there was more they needed, and Jesus told them to stay in Jerusalem and wait for it.

Although the peace of God that the disciples received at the time of their salvation was wonderful, they needed power. Jesus said, "Behold," which is the Greek word *idou*, and it means *wow*; *look*; or *see*. It carries with it *a sense of amazement*. Its use here is the equivalent of Jesus saying, "*Wow!* I am speechless regarding what you're about to receive!"

He then told them they would be "endued with power." The word "endued" is the Greek word *enduo*, meaning *to be empowered*. It also means *to clothe* and presents the idea of *sinking comfortably into a set of clothes*. The word "power" is a form of the Greek word *dunamis*, which describes *explosive, superhuman power with enormous energy that produces phenomenal, extraordinary, and unparalleled results*. This word also depicts *the force of an entire army* and was even used to signify *a force of nature*, like *a hurricane, a tornado*, or *an earthquake*.

Friend, God wants to fill you with His Holy Spirit so that you can produce *phenomenal, extraordinary, and unparalleled results*. He wants to infuse you with His explosive, superhuman power that turns you into a mighty army or a force of nature that shakes things up and blows away the enemy.

Remember, *peace* is the primary fruit of salvation, which is the first work of grace. But *power* is the primary fruit of the baptism in the Holy Spirit. Many Christians have the peace of God, but they lack the Spirit's power. This infilling of God's Spirit — the second work of grace for believers — is available to you! When you receive the baptism in the Holy Spirit, you will feel as if the full force of Heaven's army has come to live inside you!

Just as Jesus urgently instructed His disciples to wait in Jerusalem in order to receive the power of His Spirit, He is beckoning to you to receive this second work of His grace. They needed His power, and so do you!

STUDY QUESTIONS

> Study to shew thyself approved unto God, a workman that
> needeth not to be ashamed, rightly dividing the word of truth.
> — 2 Timothy 2:15

1. In Old Testament times, the Spirit of God came on individuals for a certain task and then left. Describe the reason the Spirit of God came upon Othniel (*see* Judges 3:7-11); Samson (*see* Judges 15:11-20); Saul (*see* 1 Samuel 10:1-13); and David (*see* 1 Samuel 16:10-14).
2. In John 1:32-34 something amazing happened for the *first time* ever, and it happened in the life of Jesus. What took place? According to Acts 10:38, what was Jesus able to do as a result? What did Jesus say *you* would do as you receive His strength daily (*see* John 14:12-14)?
3. *Peace* is the primary fruit of salvation. The moment we repent of our sin and receive Jesus as our Lord and Savior, we have peace with God. Explain how this peace *with* God (*see* Romans 5:1,2; Ephesians 2:13-18) is different than the peace *of* God (*see* Philippians 4:6,7; Colossians 3:15).

PRACTICAL APPLICATION

> But be ye doers of the word, and not hearers only,
> deceiving your own selves.
> — James 1:22

1. Countless Christians have experienced the gift of salvation through faith in Jesus Christ — the first work of grace. Likely you are among them. But have you also received the baptism of the Holy Spirit — the second work of grace? According to Acts 2:38 and 39, who is the baptism in the Spirit for?
2. If you *have* been filled with the Spirit, briefly share your experience and the changes that have come into your life since you were first filled. If you have not received the baptism in the Holy Spirit and would like to, read what Jesus said to do in Luke 11:9-13. (You may also call Renner Ministries and a member of our prayer team would be honored to pray with you.)

3. According to Ephesians 1:13, when we repent of our sins and make Jesus the Lord and Savior of our life, we are "sealed with that Holy Spirit of promise." Carefully reread the Greek definition of the word "sealed" (*sphragidzo*). In what ways does this meaning encourage you? How would you share this eye-opening truth with a good friend who is struggling with condemnation and fear of the future?

LESSON 12

TOPIC
The Holy Catholic (Universal) Church

SCRIPTURES
1. **1 Corinthians 12:12,13** — For as the body is one, and hath many members, and all the members of that one body, being many, are one body: so also is Christ. For by one Spirit are we all baptized into one body....
2. **Ephesians 4:4-6** — There is one body, and one Spirit, even as ye are called in one hope of your calling; one Lord, one faith, one baptism, one God and Father of all, who is above all, and through all, and in you all.

GREEK WORDS
No Greek words were shown on the TV program.

SYNOPSIS
One of the core beliefs included in The Apostles' Creed says, "I believe in… the holy catholic [universal] church." Although many have mistaken this declaration to refer to the Roman Catholic Church, it does not. Rather, it is an acknowledgment of the one, true Church — the Body of Christ from across the world, which is made up of all different backgrounds, skin colors, languages, and nationalities.

The New Testament word for "church" is *ekklesia*, and it describes who God has called us to be — *a called, separated, and prestigious assembly*. This word, taken from the *ekklesia* of the Athenian culture, pictures a distinguished group of believers who have been called out, called forth, selected, and assembled to be God's representatives in every town, city, state, or nation; a body called to make decisions that affect the atmosphere of a region. As followers of Christ, we believe in the one, true Church that God Himself is building, and the gates of hell will not prevail against it!

The emphasis of this lesson:

The Church is made up of four dominant branches: Orthodox, Catholics, Protestants, and Charismatic/Pentecostals. Altogether, there are nearly 2.7 billion Christians worldwide, which is approximately 33 percent of the world's population. Although there are many different "flavors" of Christianity, all agree on the foundational tenets of faith written in The Apostles' Creed.

A Review of The Apostles' Creed

As we've noted, the earliest form of The Apostles' Creed dates back to about 140 AD, and it was known as The Old Roman Creed. Early Church fathers called it "the rule of faith," and it preserves the undeniable core beliefs of the Christian faith. In the centuries that followed, The Apostles' Creed became a "truth filter" to strain what is being taught and determine what is and isn't authentic Christian doctrine. Today, Christians in churches around the world still quote The Apostles' Creed — you may be one of them. The question is: Do you know what you're saying? Here again is The Apostles' Creed, containing the foundational, nonnegotiable tenets of the faith:

> **I believe in God, the Father Almighty,**
> **the Creator of heaven and earth,**
> **and in Jesus Christ, His only Son, our Lord:**
> **Who was conceived of the Holy Spirit,**
> **born of the Virgin Mary,**
> **suffered under Pontius Pilate,**
> **was crucified, died, and was buried.**

He descended into hell.
The third day He arose again from the dead.
He ascended into heaven
and sits at the right hand of God the Father Almighty,
whence He shall come to judge the living and the dead.
I believe in the Holy Spirit,
the holy catholic [universal] church,
the communion of saints,
the forgiveness of sins,
the resurrection of the body,
and life everlasting. Amen.

'I Believe in… the Holy Catholic [Universal] Church'

The word "catholic" in Greek is *katholikos*, which means *universal* or *general*. Its use throughout the ages has always related to the Christian Church globally or as a whole. Thus, when we recite The Apostles' Creed and say, "I believe in the holy catholic church," we're saying that we believe and acknowledge the existence of the one, true Christian Church made up of people from all around the world who place their faith in Jesus Christ, the Son of God.

We Are ONE in Christ

Through the inspiration of the Holy Spirit, the apostle Paul wrote about the Church in First Corinthians 12, saying, "For as the body is one, and hath many members, and all the members of that one body, being many, are one body: so also is Christ. For by one Spirit are we all baptized into one body, whether we be Jews or Gentiles, whether we be bond or free; and have been all made to drink into one Spirit" (vv. 12,13).

So just as the human body has many different parts, the Church — also known as *the Body of Christ* — has many different parts. Each one is exceptionally unique and needed. Just as a human body needs all its 100 trillion cells to work together in harmony, the Church needs all its parts healthy and whole in order to carry out its full potential and purpose.

When Paul said, "For by one Spirit are we all baptized into one body" (1 Corinthians 12:13), the baptism he's talking about is what occurs the moment a person gets saved. The instant you call Jesus the Lord of your life, you are born again, and the Holy Spirit takes you and baptizes (or officially inducts and places) you into the Body of Christ. In that very moment, you become a part of God's worldwide universal Church.

That's what happens to every single person who calls Jesus Lord and is born again. The moment a person repents of their sins and surrenders their life to Jesus, the Holy Spirit baptizes him or her and places them into the body of Christ — the Church. Whether the person is of Russian descent or African, Asian or European, or any other ancestry, they're saved by the same matchless Name, washed in the same precious Blood, and placed in the same Church — the Church of the Lord Jesus Christ!

Although the Body of Christ is one, it has many diverse members. In fact, the Church is made up of a multitude of different styles, different flavors, and different expressions of faith. Yet, all who are genuinely saved are members of the universal Church. God's Word says, "There is *one* body, and *one* Spirit, even as ye are called in *one* hope of your calling; *one* Lord, *one* faith, *one* baptism, *one* God and Father of all, who is above all, and through all, and in you all" (Ephesians 4:4-6).

Can We Be Honest With Each Other?

In order to promote true unity in the Church, we must recognize and humbly admit a very common error in our thinking. Although this mindset is often on a subconscious level and goes unvoiced, we often tend to believe that our flavor of faith is the right one and the best. Rick candidly shared this about his own life:

> To be honest, when I was growing up, we were absolutely convinced that our church was the right way to be saved and to serve God, and we really didn't have much room for other denominations. I remember thinking, "Surely the Methodist and the Presbyterians are unsaved." Similarly, when my wife, Denise, was a little girl, the church she grew up in was so against Roman Catholics that she signed a commitment card in which she promised she would never marry a Roman Catholic.
>
> You can imagine our reaction when my uncle married his first wife who was a Roman Catholic. We were all simply aghast that

someone in our family would marry a Roman Catholic. Sadly, we were very narrow-minded and believed that our way was the right way, and while we knew there were other denominations, we just assumed that most of the people who were a part of them were unsaved — mainly because they were *working* for their salvation instead of receiving it by grace, through faith.

But as Denise and I began traveling around the world and ministering to people of all kinds of cultures, we learned that there are wonderful believers who are very different from us. Yet, we are all actively a part and participants of the Body of Christ.

Instead of focusing on our differences, we need to focus on where we agree. Unity of mind and heart attracts the supernatural blessings of God and is most appealing to the lost. Indeed, "How wonderful, how beautiful, when brothers and sisters get along!" (Psalm 133:1 *MSG*)

There Are Four Branches of the Christian Faith

Essentially, the Christian faith can be divided into four branches: *the Orthodox Church*, *the Catholic Church*, *the Protestant Church*, and *the Pentecostal/Charismatic Church*. Although each of these branches embrace certain doctrines that the others don't believe in, they all embrace the same core beliefs that are stated in The Apostles' Creed. Again, as we've noted, there's room for dialogue on many issues, but on the unchanging tenets of our faith, there's no room for negotiation.

Within these groups, there are many who are saved and many who are not saved. The fact is, not everyone in your church is saved. Many are authentically born again, and some are not. This is true of every Christian church across denominational lines. Many people in these groups are merely religious participants who don't really know the Bible and have never been born again. Even though they are members of a denomination, they're not members of the universal Church, because the only way you can become a member of the universal Church is by declaring Jesus is Lord and being born again. It is at this point that the Holy Spirit then places you into the real Church.

BRANCH 1: **ORTHODOX** – 260 million members worldwide

The word "Orthodox" is a compound of two Greek words: the word *orthos*, which means *straight* and describes *something correct*; and the word *doxos*, which is the word for *glory*. When these words are joined to form "Orthodox," it describes *correct worship*, and it is primarily used to describe liturgy. This word was originally derived from forms of worship from Constantinople and from the liturgy of what is called the Eastern Church. How many parts — or smaller branches — are there to the Orthodox Church? They include all of the following:

- Russian Orthodox Church
- Romanian Orthodox Church
- Church of Greece
- Serbian Orthodox Church
- Bulgarian Orthodox Church
- Ecumenical Patriarchate of Constantinople (the oldest Orthodox Church)
- Greek Orthodox Church of Antioch
- Georgian Orthodox Church
- Macedonian Orthodox Church
- Church of Cyprus
- Polish Orthodox Church
- Greek Orthodox Church of Alexandria
- Albanian Orthodox Church
- Greek Orthodox Church of Jerusalem
- Czech and Slovak Orthodox Church
- Metropolitan Church of Bessarabia (Moldova) (Romanian Patriarchate)
- Finnish Orthodox Church (Ecumenical Patriarchate)
- Estonian Orthodox Church (Ecumenical Patriarchate)
- Russian Orthodox Church Outside Russia
- Ukrainian Orthodox Church (Moscow Patriarchate)

- Metropolitan Church of Moldova (Moscow Patriarchate)
- Estonian Orthodox Church (Moscow Patriarchate)
- Chinese Orthodox Church (Moscow Patriarchate)
- Japanese Orthodox Church (Moscow Patriarchate)
- Latvian Orthodox Church (Moscow Patriarchate)
- Orthodox Church of Ukraine
- Belarusian Orthodox Church
- Orthodox Church of Greece (Holy Synod in Resistance)
- Old Calendar Bulgarian Orthodox Church
- Orthodox Church in Italy
- Old Calendarist Romanian Orthodox Church
- Montenegrin Orthodox Church
- Old Believers
- Greek Old Calendarists
- True Orthodox Church
- Evangelical Orthodox Church
- Turkish Orthodox Patriarchate
- Ethiopian Orthodox Tewahedo Church
- Coptic Orthodox Church
- Armenian Apostolic Church
- Holy See of Cilicia
- Armenian Patriarchate of Constantinople
- Armenian Patriarchate of Jerusalem
- Eritrean Orthodox Church
- Orthodox Syrian Church
- Syriac Orthodox Church

- Jacobite Syrian Christian Orthodox Church
- French Coptic Orthodox Church
- Malabar Independent Syrian Church
- British Orthodox Church
- Orthodox Church in America

Here we see more than 50 different flavors of the Orthodox Church, and within these churches there are genuine born-again believers and nonbelievers.

BRANCH 2: **CATHOLIC** – 1.3 billion members worldwide

As we noted, the word "catholic" means *universal*. Although when most people hear the word "catholic," they think of the Roman Catholic Church and the Vatican (its headquarters in the city of Rome), but the Catholic Church also includes:

- Roman Catholic Church
- Roman Catholic Ukrainian Church
- Greek Catholic Church
- Melkite Greek Catholic Church
- Romanian Greek Catholic Church
- Ruthenian Greek Catholic Church
- Hungarian Greek Catholic Church
- Slovak Greek Catholic Church
- Belarusian Greek Catholic Church
- Italo-Albanian Catholic Church
- Greek Catholic Church of Croatia and Serbia
- Georgian Byzantine Catholic Church
- Albanian Greek Catholic Church
- Russian Greek Catholic Church
- Greek Byzantine Catholic Church

- Macedonian Greek Catholic Church
- Bulgarian Greek Catholic Church
- Syro-Malabar Church
- Chaldean Catholic Church
- Maronite Catholic Church
- Syro-Malankara Catholic Church
- Syriac Catholic Church
- Armenian Catholic Church
- Coptic Catholic Church
- Eritrean Catholic Church
- Ethiopian Catholic Church
- Philippine Independent Catholic Church
- Chinese Patriotic Catholic Association
- Apostolic Catholic Church
- Traditionalist Mexican-American Catholic Church
- Brazilian Catholic Apostolic Church
- Old Catholic Church
- Polish National Catholic Church
- Palmarian Catholic Church

Here we see 34 different flavors of the Catholic Church, and within these churches there are genuine born-again believers and nonbelievers.

BRANCH 3: **PROTESTANT** – 1 billion members worldwide

The word "Protestant" means *to protest*, and it is a branch of Christianity that emerged as a result of the revelation that salvation is by faith alone. This group was formed by those who first protested against many doctrinal points in the Roman Catholic Church. Thus, they were first called "Protestants." The biggest difference in belief that the Protestants had — and still have — is that salvation is solely by the grace of God, through faith. The Protestant Church includes:

Historical Protestantism – 560 million members worldwide

- Anglicans
- Baptists
- Lutherans
- Presbyterians (and its various forms)
- Reformed Churches
- Congregationalists
- Methodists (and its various forms)
- Restorationists
- Anabaptists
- Plymouth Brethren
- Hussites

Modern Protestantism – 400-500 million members worldwide

- African churches
- Chinese Patriotic Christian Churches
- New Apostolic Church
- Unaffiliated Churches
- Messianic Judaism
- Eastern Protestant Christianity
- Plus — other Protestant groups that do not fit into the above categories

Here we see numerous different flavors of the Protestant Church, and within these churches there are genuine born-again believers and nonbelievers.

BRANCH 4: **PENTECOSTAL/CHARISMATIC** – 700 million members worldwide

The number of Pentecostal/Charismatic believers is enormous. Again, there are approximately 260 million Orthodox believers; 1.3 billion Catholics; 1 billion Protestants; and 700 million Pentecostals/Charismatics. In total, there are 2.7 billion Christians in the world, which means approximately 33 percent of the world's population are Christians.

The fact that nearly 700 million believers claim to be Pentecostal/Charismatic means that 1 out of every 4 Christians is Pentecostal/Charismatic. This is an amazing statistic considering that this movement started in contemporary history — not much more than 100 years ago.

The Charismatic movement is desperately needed to help advance the cause of Christ to the ends of the earth. It is a God-sent movement to energize the Church with the power of the Holy Spirit. The Church must have the supernatural work — and the supernatural equipment — of the Holy Spirit to accomplish the Christ-commissioned task of reaching the world with the Gospel before Jesus returns.

NOW MORE THAN EVER….

It is imperative that Christian leaders step forward in this hour to do everything they can to keep the Church on track and doctrinally anchored in Scripture. Remember, in First Timothy 4:1, the Holy Spirit prophesied that many will veer off track in the last days. That's why we're studying The Apostles' Creed — to know and be grounded in the nonnegotiable truths of the Christian faith.

Friend, you need to be in a solid Christian church…

- That holds firmly to the Word of God.
- That holds firmly to the belief that people need to be saved through faith in Jesus.
- That holds firmly to a belief and practice of the power of the Holy Spirit.

Yes, the Church of the Lord Jesus Christ is real — and it's huge! Nevertheless, all four branches, despite their many differences, are all in agreement with what is written in The Apostles' Creed. In our next lesson, we will explore what the apostles meant regarding the statement, "I believe in…the communion of saints."

STUDY QUESTIONS

> Study to shew thyself approved unto God, a workman that needeth not to be ashamed, rightly dividing the word of truth.
> — 2 Timothy 2:15

1. Thinking back to Paul's example of the Church as a physical body, how should we interact with other parts of the Body of Christ that serve different functions and look different than we do — whether in worship, doctrine, or even personality? Take some time to carefully read through First Corinthians 12 as you answer this question and write what the Holy Spirit speaks to you.
2. In historical context, the Jews had always been taught strict rules about what they could and couldn't touch, eat, or with whom they could associate. Most of these laws were for their protection, but they also eventually bred a sense of contempt for anyone and anything different than themselves. What did God show Peter about the new perspective we are to have as believers regarding other believers — including their backgrounds and styles of worship that are different from what we grew up with? (Consider God's revelation to Peter in Acts 10.)

PRACTICAL APPLICATION

> But be ye doers of the word, and not hearers only, deceiving your own selves.
> — James 1:22

1. What new facts did you learn about your "flavor" of faith and Christianity in general in this lesson?
2. How do the four different branches of the Church shed light on how things are organized? Which branch do you come from, and which branch are you currently a part of?
3. What negative experiences have you had with people and churches that belonged to a different branch than you? Have you had any positive ones with those from a different affiliation? If so, what are they and how have they stretched you and helped you grow?
4. Either way, it's valuable to look back, remember, and learn from them. Take time to celebrate the good memories and invite the Holy Spirit to heal your heart from the hurtful ones. He wants to give you the

discernment you need to stay spiritually sound and the freedom to connect with Him in new, life-giving ways.

LESSON 13

TOPIC
The Communion of Saints

SCRIPTURES

1. **Exodus 3:1-5** — Now Moses kept the flock of Jethro his father in law, the priest of Midian: and he led the flock to the backside of the desert, and came to the mountain of God, even to Horeb. And the angel of the Lord appeared unto him in a flame of fire out of the midst of a bush: and he looked, and, behold, the bush burned with fire, and the bush was not consumed. And Moses said, I will now turn aside, and see this great sight, why the bush is not burnt. And when the Lord saw that he turned aside to see, God called unto him out of the midst of the bush, and said, Moses, Moses. And he said, Here am I. And he said, Draw not nigh hither: put off thy shoes from off thy feet, for the place whereon thou standest is holy ground.

2. **Romans 1:7** — To all that be in Rome, beloved of God, called to be saints....

3. **1 Corinthians 6:9-11** — Know ye not that the unrighteous shall not inherit the kingdom of God? Be not deceived: neither fornicators, nor idolaters, nor adulterers, nor effeminate, nor abusers of themselves with mankind, nor thieves, nor covetous, nor drunkards, nor revilers, nor extortioners, shall inherit the kingdom of God. And such were some of you: but ye are washed, but ye are sanctified, but ye are justified in the name of the Lord Jesus, and by the Spirit of our God.

4. **Hebrews 12:22,23** — But ye are come unto mount Sion, and unto the city of the living God, the heavenly Jerusalem, and to an innumerable company of angels, to the general assembly and church of the firstborn, which are written in heaven, and to God the Judge of all, and to the spirits of just men made perfect.

GREEK WORDS

1. "holy" — ἅγιος (*hagios*): describes something that, even though it was once common, has now become separated, consecrated, holy, and sacred — never again to be regarded or used in a common way; anything "holy" is in a category that is separate and sacred from other things
2. "washed" — ἀπολούω (*apolouo*): a compound of the preposition ἀπό (*apo*) and λούω (*louo*); the preposition ἀπό (*apo*) means from and away, as in a separation; the word λούω (*louo*) means to bathe and to cleanse; as a compound, one whose former filth has been cleansed off of him; he is cleansed so thoroughly that he is completely separated from his past condition
3. "sanctified" — ἁγιάζω (*hagiadzo*): from ἅγιος (*hagios*), which describes something that, even though it was once common, has now become separated, consecrated, holy, and sacred — never again to be regarded or used in a common way; anything "holy" is in a category that is separate and sacred from other things; however, ἁγιάζω (*hagiadzo*) depicts the process by which one is made holy
4. "justified" — δικαιόω (*dikaioo*): one who is legally approved; legally declared just, right, or righteous; depicts one who has had all charges of guilt against him permanently removed

SYNOPSIS

Life is about relationships. We were not designed to live alone but in meaningful fellowship with one another. The Bible refers to this as *the communion of saints*, and this empowering companionship with fellow believers is meant to be enjoyed both in this life and in the life to come. Indeed, "As iron sharpens iron, so one person sharpens another" (Proverbs 27:17 *NASB*). The communion of the saints is another major statement of faith found in The Apostles' Creed.

The emphasis of this lesson:

The concept of holiness is first introduced to us in the story of Moses and his encounter with God on the "holy" mount. The word "holy" describes something *set apart*, *separated*, *consecrated*, and *sacred*. Examples of what God calls holy include the holy mount where He met Moses, His Holy Word, and us — His holy people He calls "saints."

A Review of The Apostles' Creed

As we've seen, the earliest form of The Apostles' Creed was known as The Old Roman Creed, which dates back to about 140 AD. In 390 AD, it was revised, which is the version we have today, and the Early Church fathers called it "the rule of faith." It contains the indisputable core beliefs of the Christian faith. For centuries since then, The Apostles' Creed became a "truth filter" to help determine what is and isn't authentic Christian doctrine. Today, we, too, can learn and utilize The Apostles' Creed to help us determine what is and isn't sound Christian truth. Here again is The Apostles' Creed:

> I believe in God, the Father Almighty,
> the Creator of heaven and earth,
> and in Jesus Christ, His only Son, our Lord:
> Who was conceived of the Holy Spirit,
> born of the Virgin Mary,
> suffered under Pontius Pilate,
> was crucified, died, and was buried.
> He descended into hell.
> The third day He arose again from the dead.
> He ascended into heaven
> and sits at the right hand of God the Father Almighty,
> whence He shall come to judge the living and the dead.
> I believe in the Holy Spirit,
> the holy catholic [universal] church,
> the communion of saints,
> the forgiveness of sins,
> the resurrection of the body,
> and life everlasting. Amen.

Moses Encountered God on 'Holy Ground'

The next tenet of The Apostles' Creed we will look at is "I Believe in… the communion of saints." To help you understand the meaning of the word *saint*, let's journey back in time to a defining moment recorded in Exodus 3. There Moses had his encounter with God at the site of a burning bush — a bush that burned but was not consumed by the fire. In Exodus 3:1-5 the Bible says:

> **Now Moses kept the flock of Jethro his father in law, the priest of Midian: and he led the flock to the backside of the desert, and came to the mountain of God, even to Horeb.**
>
> **And the angel of the Lord appeared unto him in a flame of fire out of the midst of a bush: and he looked, and, behold, the bush burned with fire, and the bush was not consumed.**
>
> **And Moses said, I will now turn aside, and see this great sight, why the bush is not burnt.**
>
> **And when the Lord saw that he turned aside to see, God called unto him out of the midst of the bush, and said, Moses, Moses. And he said, Here am I.**
>
> **And he said, Draw not nigh hither: put off thy shoes from off thy feet, for the place whereon thou standest is holy ground.**

Scripture says Moses saw the burning bush as a "great sight" — something that stunned and amazed him because he had never witnessed anything like it. In that hallowed moment, he crossed the threshold that separated the natural realm from the realm that God called "holy." The physical location that Moses entered at that moment was so sacred to God that He commanded Moses to remove his shoes so he wouldn't carry the contamination of the earth into this holy place that had become God's sanctuary.

Notice the word "holy" in Exodus 3:5. It is the word *hagia* in the Old Testament Greek Septuagint, a form of the word *hagios*. From this point forward throughout the Bible, this word *hagios* is used to denote *the holiness of God*, *the holy presence of God*, or *anything that God deems to be holy*. The spot where Moses stood was a place on this earth where God dwelt that was so holy, no worldly contamination was permitted there.

Understanding the Meaning of 'Holy'

In both the Old Testament Greek Septuagint and in the Greek New Testament, the Greek word for "holy" is translated from various forms of this Greek word *hagios*, which is one of the most important words in the entire Bible. This word "holy," the word *hagios*, describes something that, even though it was once common, has now become *separated, consecrated, holy*, and *sacred* — never again to be regarded or used in a common way. Anything "holy" is in a category that is separate and sacred from other things.

God's written Word is called the Holy Bible. A simple illustration of this word "holy" is connected to Scripture itself. The *King James* translators were some of the earliest to give the Bible's full name as the *Holy Bible*. The word "Bible" is a translation of the Greek word *biblios*, which simply means *book, books*, or *a scroll of writing*.

As mentioned earlier, the word "holy" — the Greek word *hagios* — means *separated, consecrated, holy, sacred*, or *never to be regarded or used in a common way*. Thus, anything that is "holy" is in a category that is separate and sacred from other things. That means the *Holy Bible* is a special book that is *consecrated, separated*, and *set apart* from all other books. The *Holy Bible* is so different that no other book in the world compares to it.

If you walk into a library, you will probably find a copy of the *Holy Bible* on its shelves. But even though it is located in a library full of books, the word "holy" in the name "Holy Bible" signifies that it is in a category all by itself. And every time you call that precious Book by its name, you're affirming that it is like no other book… that it is *set apart* into a special, *consecrated, holy category* and that it is different from all the other books in the library.

The mountain where Moses met God was holy. That day on Mount Horeb when Moses approached the burning bush, God told him to remove his shoes because he was standing on "holy" ground. The fact that the word "holy" is a translation of the Greek word *hagios* tells us that God consecrated and sanctified that particular spot on the mountain.

Now if you had been there and looked at that mountain, you would have thought it looked no different from other mountains in the region. Though there was nothing particularly unique about that mountain in terms of its appearance compared to other mountains, God's presence had touched it. And in that moment, His divine presence supernaturally separated that mountain from all other mountains and set it apart into a *holy* category.

It became so sacred at that moment that it became known as the *holy mount*. Although it was nestled as one mountain in the midst of an entire mountain range of normal mountains, it ceased to be normal from that day forward. God's presence had forever changed its status.

What Is a 'Saint'?

As you consider the word "holy," keep in mind these ideas of *separation*, *consecration*, and *being placed into a unique category*. The apostle Paul used this concept throughout his epistles in a powerful way to describe us as believers. For instance, when he wrote to the Christians in Rome — as well as to all believers everywhere — he began his letter in Romans 1:7 by saying, "To all that be in Rome, beloved of God, called to be saints…."

When people see or hear the word "saints," they sometimes imagine individuals with halos above their heads, but that is not what this word is referring to. The word translated "saints" here is actually a form of the Greek word *hagios*, the same word translated as "holy" in most places in the Bible. That said, a "saint" (*hagios*) describes someone that, even though once common, has now become *separated*, *consecrated*, *holy*, and *sacred* — *never again to be regarded or used in a common way*. Thus, as "saints," we are in a category that is separate and sacred from other things.

Paul used the word *hagios* — translated here and in other places as "saints" — to describe Christians. Before coming to Christ, we were just regular human beings like everyone else. But when the blood of Jesus cleansed us and the Holy Spirit moved into our hearts, that divine presence set us apart and made us so different that God immediately saw us in a special, holy light that was different from unsaved people. We are called to be different, sanctified, and in a separate category from the rest of the world — a category called *holy*.

Second Corinthians 5:17 and 21 teaches that we were reconciled to God the instant we received Jesus as Savior and Lord and the Spirit of God came to live in our hearts. At that moment, God judicially reckoned us to be righteous. In a fraction of a split second, quicker than the mind can comprehend, the Holy Spirit's presence within us removed us from the category of unregenerate human beings and moved us over into the special category of *set-apart*, *consecrated*, and *marked-off holy* beings created in God's own image.

You and Mount Horeb Have Something in Common

If you're a believer, you might outwardly look like any other human being, but you're *not* like everyone else. Just as the presence of God came down on Mount Horeb and made it holy, the moment the blood of Jesus washed you and the Holy Spirit entered your spirit, God separated you, consecrated you, and set you apart for Himself. You are the home of the Holy Spirit — and as such, you are holy.

God justified us and made us to be righteous by faith — and in that act, we moved over into a new category of human beings! We might look like regular people, but there is nothing regular about us. As new creations who are separated into a higher, holy category, God calls us to adjust our thinking to His holy written Word and behave accordingly. We should no longer think or act as we once did because we are not who we once were. We are new, different, and holy. That means we need to think differently, talk differently, and act differently, and we will do this more and more as we spend regular time with God.

The Spirit of God lives in us, and just as God's holy presence sanctified the physical location of the burning bush on Mount Horeb, His divine presence in our lives has set perimeters around us that separates us from the rest of the world. We are holy ground! All of this is in the word "saint" used in Romans 1:7 and in other places throughout the New Testament.

As 'Saints,' We Are Never To Be Regarded As We Once Were

As the apostle Paul was bringing instruction to the believers at Corinth, he said, "Know ye not that the unrighteous shall not inherit the kingdom of God? Be not deceived: neither fornicators, nor idolaters, nor adulterers, nor effeminate, nor abusers of themselves with mankind, nor thieves, nor covetous, nor drunkards, nor revilers, nor extortioners, shall inherit the kingdom of God. And such were some of you: but ye are washed, but ye are sanctified, but ye are justified in the name of the Lord Jesus, and by the Spirit of our God" (1 Corinthians 6:9-11).

We have been *washed*. There are three very important words in this passage, and the first one is "washed." It is the Greek word *apolouo*, which is a compound of the preposition *apo* and the word *louo*. The preposition *apo* means *from and away*, as in *a separation*; and the word *louo* means *to* *bathe* and *to cleanse*. When compounded to form *apolouo*, it means *one whose former filth has been cleansed off him*. He is cleansed so thoroughly that he is completely separated from his past condition.

We have been *sanctified*. In addition to being washed, Paul said these believers were "sanctified," which is a translation of the Greek word *hagiadzo*, from the word *hagios*, the word for "holy" that we've been studying. Again, it describes something that, even though it was once common, has now become *separated*, *consecrated*, *holy*, and *sacred* — never again to be regarded or used in a common way. Anything "holy" is in a category that is separate and sacred from other things. When *hagios* takes on the form *hagiadzo*, it depicts *the process by which one is made holy*.

We have been *justified*. The third word Paul used in this passage to explain what happens when we are born again is the word "justified." This word is taken from the Greek word *dikaioo*, which describes *one who is legally approved* or *one legally declared just, right, or righteous*. It depicts *one who has had all charges of guilt against him permanently removed*.

Washed, *sanctified*, and *justified* are all words that describe what God has done in your life as you put your faith in the finished work of Christ. In fact, these words describe all believers of all generations. The writer of Hebrews referred to this new status. He wrote, "But ye are come unto mount Zion, and unto the city of the living God, the heavenly Jerusalem, and to an innumerable company of angels, to the general assembly and church of the firstborn, which are written in heaven, and to God the Judge of all, and to the spirits of just men made perfect" (Hebrews 12:22,23).

Notice the phrase "the general assembly and church of the firstborn, which are in heaven." This is *the communion of the saints* referred to in The Apostles' Creed. These are those who've been washed in the blood of Jesus, sanctified by His Holy Spirit, and justified by the Father. The communion of the saints is a precious gift from God — not only to be celebrated in Heaven but also to be experienced here on earth in our day-to-day fellowship with our brothers and sisters in Christ.

In our next lesson, we'll examine the indescribable gift of the forgiveness of sins.

STUDY QUESTIONS

> **Study to shew thyself approved** unto God, a workman that
> **needeth not to** be ashamed, rightly dividing the word of truth.
> — 2 Timothy 2:15

1. The Holy Bible is so different that no other book in the world compares to it. It is *separated, consecrated, holy, sacred*, and *never to be regarded or used in a common way*. What do these passages say about God's Word that highlights the fact it is in a holy class all by itself?

   - Hebrews 4:12
   - James 1:21-25
   - 2 Timothy 3:15-17

2. In light of the fact that we've been made *holy* through faith in Christ's finished work on the Cross, how should that affect the way we live on a daily basis? Take a look at what God has to say about it in Romans 12:1,2; Ephesians 4:17-32; and Hebrews 12:1,2.

3. According to the documented accounts in Second Samuel 6:1-12; Second Kings 13:20,21; Acts 5:15,16; and Acts 19:11 and 12, what kind of things happened when ordinary people came into contact with *holy* people and *holy* things? What is the Holy Spirit speaking to you to do to prepare yourself as one of His saints — His holy ones — that exhibits His extraordinary power? (*Consider* Second Timothy 2:20-22.)

PRACTICAL APPLICATION

> **But be ye doers of the word, and not hearers only,**
> **deceiving your own selves.**
> — James 1:22

1. In your own words, describe what it means to be one of God's "saints." How does He see you?

2. Knowing that we're called to be holy, separate, and different from the rest of the world, it's absolutely crucial that we intentionally support and come together with fellow believers as the communion of saints (*see* Hebrews 10:25). What do you think would change in your life if you had solid, sincere believers around to encourage and lift you up?

What's keeping you from prayerfully reaching out and making some new, healthy God-connections with others?
3. Just like Moses had Mount Horeb, each of us has at least one place where we have encountered God. What is your "holy ground"? Where do you have one or more memories or moments of making an unforgettable connection with God? Ask Him to help you keep it fresh in your mind and heart.

LESSON 14

TOPIC

The Forgiveness of Sin

SCRIPTURES

1. **Psalm 65:3** — Iniquities prevail against me: as for our transgressions, thou shalt purge them away.
2. **Psalm 103:2,3** — Bless the Lord, O my soul, and forget not all his benefits; Who forgiveth all thine iniquities….
3. **Psalm 103:12** — As far as the east is from the west, so far hath he removed our transgressions from us.
4. **Acts 3:19** — Repent ye therefore, and be converted, that your sins may be blotted out….
5. **Ephesians 1:7** — In whom we have redemption through his blood, the forgiveness of sins, according to the riches of his grace.
6. **Colossians 1:13,14** — Who hath delivered us from the power of darkness, and hath translated us into the kingdom of his dear Son: In whom we have redemption through his blood, even the forgiveness of sins.
7. **1 John 1:9** — If we confess our sins, he is faithful and just to forgive us our sins, and to cleanse us from all unrighteousness.
8. **1 John 2:12** — I write unto you, little children, because your sins are forgiven you for his name's sake.
9. **Hebrews 9:14** — How much more shall the blood of Christ, who through the eternal Spirit offered himself without spot to God, purge your conscience from dead works to serve the living God?

GREEK WORDS

1. "repent" — μετανοέω (*metanoeo*): a change of mind that results in a complete, radical, total change of behavior; a decision to completely change or to entirely turn around in the way that one is thinking, believing, or living; a total transformation affecting every part of a person's life, both inside and outside, resulting in a behavioral change
2. "converted" — ἐπιστρέφω (*epistrepho*): a compound of the preposition ἐπί (*epi*) and the word στρέφω (*strepho*); the preposition ἐπί (*epi*) is used as an intensifier, and the word στρέφω (*strepho*) means to change, turn, or switch and pictures a radical change or turn-around
3. "blotted out" — ἐξαλείφω (*exsaleipho*): to rub out, to cancel, to completely remove, to permanently wipe away, or to obliterate
4. "through" — διά (*dia*): through, by, or on account of; speaks of the agency of this action, which is by the blood of Jesus
5. "forgiveness" — ἄφεσις (*aphesis*): from ἀφίημι (*aphiemi*); to forgive, to permanently dismiss, or to release; to set free; to let go; to discharge; to send away; to liberate completely; to forfeit one's right to ever bring it up again; used in New Testament times in reference to canceling a debt or releasing someone from the obligation of a contract, a commitment, or a promise; to forfeit any right to hold a person captive to a previous commitment or wrong he has committed; to irretrievably remove
6. "according to" — κατά (*kata*): a preposition which here pictures a dominating or subjugating force; could be translated being dominated by
7. "riches" — πλοῦτος (*ploutos*): immense wealth or riches beyond imagination; one who possesses riches so immense that they are seemingly immeasurable; abundant or measureless resources; wealth so great it cannot be tabulated; used by Plato to say no one was richer than legendary King Midas
8. "delivered" — ῥύομαι (*rhuomai*): to rescue, to deliver, to snatch, or to drag out of danger; to save in the nick of time; a rescue operation intended to snatch a person out of physical or spiritual peril; intervention
9. "from" — ἐκ (*ek*): out, out from, or away from; where we get the word exit
10. "power" — ἐξουσία (*exousia*): authority or influence
11. "translated" — μεθίστημι (*methistemi*): to transfer; to remove from one place and transfer to another place; to translate

12. "confess" — ὁμολογέω (*homologeo*): to agree, affirm, confess, or profess; to say the same thing; to be in alignment with another's thoughts and words
13. "forgive" — ἄφεσις (*aphesis*): from ἀφίημι (*aphiemi*); to forgive, to permanently dismiss, or to release; to set free; to let go; to discharge; to send away; to liberate completely; to forfeit one's right to ever bring it up again; used in New Testament times in reference to canceling a debt or releasing someone from the obligation of a contract, a commitment, or a promise; to forfeit any right to hold a person captive to a previous commitment or wrong he has committed; to irretrievably remove
14. "cleanse" — καθαρίζω (*katharidzo*): from καθαρός (*katharos*); clean, purged, pure, or unstained; hence, guiltless, innocent, and upright
15. "from" — ἀπό (*apo*): a preposition that means from, as away from, and carries the idea of separation
16. "forgiven" — ἄφεσις (*aphesis*): from ἀφίημι (*aphiemi*); to forgive, to permanently dismiss, or to release; to set free; to let go; to discharge; to send away; to liberate completely; to forfeit one's right to ever bring it up again; used in New Testament times in reference to canceling a debt or releasing someone from the obligation of a contract, a commitment, or a promise; to forfeit any right to hold a person captive to a previous commitment or wrong he has committed; to irretrievably remove
17. "conscience" — συνείδησις (*suneidesis*): inward thoughts; one's self-consideration; self-judgment

SYNOPSIS

Have you ever done wrong and *not* dealt with your sin? King David did, and he tells us what happened to him as a result. He said, "When I refused to confess my sin, my body wasted away, and I groaned all day long. Day and night your hand [God] of discipline was heavy on me. My strength evaporated like water in the summer heat" (Psalm 32:3,4 *NLT*).

What happened when David humbled himself and asked the Lord for forgiveness? He said, "Finally, I confessed all my sins to you and stopped trying to hide my guilt. I said to myself, 'I will confess my rebellion to the Lord.' And you forgave me! All my guilt is gone" (Psalm 32:5 *NLT*). Indeed, God's Word is true when it says, "…What *joy* for those whose record the Lord has cleared of guilt, whose lives are lived in complete honesty!" (Psalm 32:2 *NLT*)

Friend, the forgiveness of sin is available to you through the precious blood of Jesus! This statement of faith is another core belief preserved in The Apostles' Creed and a recurring truth expressed throughout the New Testament.

The emphasis of this lesson:

When God forgives our sin, He permanently dismisses it, forfeiting His right to ever bring it up again. To receive His forgiveness, we must confess and repent of our sins. When we truly repent, we experience a total transformation affecting every part of our life, both inside and out. Repentance makes a way for our sins to be completely removed and obliterated from our lives, and this is all made possible through the precious blood of Jesus.

A Review of The Apostles' Creed

The Apostles' Creed is one of the earliest creeds of the Church. The first version was known as The Old Roman Creed, which dates to about 140 AD. The version we have today is a revision of the original and dates to 390 AD. The Early Church fathers called The Apostles' Creed "the rule of faith," as it contains the irrefutable core beliefs of the Christian faith. It has served as a "truth filter" for centuries, helping believers determine what is and isn't authentic Christian doctrine. Today, churches across the globe continue to recite The Apostles' Creed as a regular part of their worship experience. When said from the heart, this creed reinforces what we believe and unites us with others of like precious faith. Here again is The Apostles' Creed:

I believe in God, the Father Almighty,
the Creator of heaven and earth,
and in Jesus Christ, His only Son, our Lord:
Who was conceived of the Holy Spirit,
born of the Virgin Mary,
suffered under Pontius Pilate,
was crucified, died, and was buried.
He descended into hell.

> The third day He arose again from the dead.
> He ascended into heaven
> and sits at the right hand of God the Father Almighty,
> whence He shall come to judge the living and the dead.
> I believe in the Holy Spirit,
> the holy catholic [universal] church,
> the communion of saints,
> the forgiveness of sins,
> the resurrection of the body,
> and life everlasting. Amen.

'I Believe in… the Forgiveness of Sins'

David was a man after God's heart. Yet, he was also a man who experienced the weight of his own sin. After ignoring his sinful behavior of lying, adultery, and murder, David finally came clean with God and repented of his sins. It was at that time he wrote Psalm 32, which says, "Oh, what joy for those whose disobedience is forgiven, whose sin is put out of sight!" (v. 1 *NLT*)

Later, when David was going through a hard time, he spoke to himself and said, "Bless the Lord, O my soul, and forget not all his benefits, who forgiveth all thine iniquities; who healeth all thy diseases (Psalm 103:2,3). Instead of thinking and talking about all the difficulties he was dealing with, David literally spoke to his soul and said, "Soul, bless the Lord! Remember and don't forget all of His blessings — especially His willingness to forgive sin and heal us from all diseases."

In Psalm 103:12, David exclaims just how extensive God's forgiveness is. He said, "As far as the east is from the west, so far hath he removed our transgressions from us." Interestingly, if you were to walk east and keep walking east, you'd never reach west, because they never meet. God uses this expression to tell us that when He forgives our sin, He removes it so far away from us it cannot be measured!

Micah 7:19 in the *Good News Translation* says, "You will be merciful to us once again. You will trample our sins underfoot and send them to the bottom of the sea!" Does God actually forget our sins? No. He just chooses — on purpose — not to remember them. Without question, there is NO ONE like our God!

What Does the New Testament Say About Forgiveness?

When we come to Acts 3, we find that Peter and John were used by God to bring supernatural healing to a lame beggar. As onlookers began to gather at the scene, Peter seized the opportunity to preach the Gospel. As he made his appeal for people to get right with God, he said, "Repent ye therefore, and be converted, that your sins may be blotted out…" (Acts 3:19).

Notice the word "repent" here as it is very important. It is the Greek word *metanoeo*, and it describes *a change of mind that results in a complete, radical, total change of behavior*. It is *a decision to completely change or to entirely turn around in the way that one is thinking, believing, or living*. When a person truly repents, he or she experiences *a total transformation affecting every part of their life, both inside and outside, resulting in a behavioral change*.

It should be noted that the word "repent" primarily has to do with the mind. It's a willful admission that what you've done is wrong, and you decide to change and turn in the right direction. This means you don't have to cry or even feel sorry to repent. You just need to decide to do things God's way and not your own way or the world's way. True repentance produces an internal change of thinking and an external change in behavior, a movement toward doing things God's way.

Peter said, "Repent ye therefore, and be converted…" (Acts 3:19). In Greek, the word "converted" is *epistrepho*, a compound of the preposition *epi* and the word *strepho*. The preposition *epi* is used as *an intensifier*, and the word *strepho* means *to change*, *turn*, or *switch*. It pictures *a radical change or turn-around*. When one truly repents from the heart, the Bible says his sins will be "blotted out." This phrase is a translation of the Greek word *exsaleipho*, which means *to rub out*, *to cancel*, *to completely remove*, *to permanently wipe away*, or *to obliterate*. Repentance makes a way for our sins to be completely removed and obliterated from our lives.

Forgiveness of Sin Is Through Jesus' Blood

The reason we have forgiveness today is because of Christ's finished work on the Cross. In Ephesians 1:7, Paul writes, "In whom we have redemption through his blood, the forgiveness of sins, according to the riches of his grace." There are four significant words you need to know in this verse, and the first one is the word "through." It is the Greek word *dia*, meaning *through*, *by*, or *on account of*. This word *dia* speaks of the agency of this action, which is the blood of Jesus. Hence, we could translate this verse to read, "In Christ Jesus, we have redemption *through* his blood, *by* His blood, *on account of* His blood…."

It is also through, by, and on account of Jesus' blood that we have *forgiveness of sins*. The word "forgiveness" in this verse is the Greek word *aphesis*, which is from the word *aphiemi*, meaning *to forgive*. Moreover, it means *to permanently dismiss*; *to release*; *to set free*; *to let go*; *to discharge*; *to send away*; or *to liberate completely*. Equally important, it means *to forfeit one's right to ever bring it up again*. This word *aphiemi* was used in New Testament times in reference to canceling a debt or releasing someone from the obligation of a contract, commitment, or promise. Likewise, it indicates a willingness to forfeit any right to hold a person captive to a previous commitment or wrong he has committed. It carries the idea of *irretrievably removing something*.

The use of this word *aphiemi* — translated here as "forgiveness" — means once God has forgiven you of your sin, He has let it go and He'll never bring it up again. It is gone from the mind of God. Paul says we receive the forgiveness of sins "…according to the riches of his grace" (Ephesians 1:7). The phrase "according to" is a translation of the Greek word *kata*, a preposition which here pictures *a dominating or subjugating force*. Thus, this part of the verse could be translated, "We have forgiveness of sins, being dominated by and subjugated by the riches of his grace."

This brings us to the word "riches," which is the Greek word *ploutos*. It describes *immense wealth* or *riches beyond imagination*. It depicts *one who possesses riches so immense that they are seemingly immeasurable*. This word *ploutos* indicates *abundant or measureless resources*; *wealth so great it cannot be tabulated*. Interestingly, this is the very word used by Plato to say no one was richer than legendary King Midas. The Holy Spirit prompted Paul to use this word to tell us that God has so much grace it can't be tabulated! And it is His immeasurable grace that dominates our lives and brings forgiveness.

We've Been Delivered From Darkness to Light

To all this, Paul adds, "[God] Who hath delivered us from the power of darkness, and hath translated us into the kingdom of his dear Son" (Colossians 1:13). The word for "delivered" here is the unique Greek word *rhuomai*, which means *to rescue, to deliver, to snatch*, or *to drag out of danger*. It carries the idea of *saving someone in the nick of time*. It pictures a rescue operation intended to snatch a person out of physical or spiritual peril. Hence, Colossians 1:13 depicts God's divine intervention.

Through the precious blood of Jesus, God divinely intervened in our life and snatched us from the power of darkness. The word "from" in Colossians 1:13 is the Greek word *ek*, which means *out, out from*, or *away from*. It is where we get the word *exit*, and its use here means that your salvation gave you an *exit* from the power of darkness and translated you into the kingdom of God's dear Son.

The word "power" here is the Greek word *exousia*, which means *authority* or *influence*. Thus, God has rescued and snatched us up away from the *authority* and *influence* of darkness. At the same time, He has *translated* us into the kingdom of His dear Son. In Greek, the word "translated" is *methistemi*, and it means *to transfer* or *to remove from one place and transfer to another place*. Through the atoning power of Jesus' blood, God literally removed you from the kingdom of darkness and placed you into the kingdom of His dear Son. That is what this word "translated" means.

Paul goes on to say that in Jesus, "…We have redemption through his blood, even the forgiveness of sins" (Colossians 1:14). The word "through" is again the Greek word *dia*, meaning *through, by*, or *on account of*. This speaks of the agency of this action, which is by the blood of Jesus. Therefore, just as we saw earlier in Ephesians 1:7, these words in Colossians 1:14 could be translated, "In Christ, we have redemption *through* his blood, *by* His blood, *on account of* His blood — even the forgiveness of sins." Without the blood that Jesus willingly shed, we could not be redeemed or forgiven.

The word "forgiveness" in Colossians 1:14 is the same word we saw in Ephesians 1:7 — the Greek word *aphesis*, from the word *aphiemi*. Again, it means *to forgive, to permanently dismiss*, or *to release*. It denotes one who chooses *to set free, let go, discharge, send away*, or *liberate completely*. In addition, it means *to forfeit one's right to ever bring it up again*. In New Testament times, this word *aphiemi* was used in reference to canceling a debt or releasing someone from the obligation of a contract, commitment, or promise; to irretrievably remove. Moreover, it meant forfeiting any right to hold a person captive to a previous commitment or wrong he had committed. The Holy Spirit's use of this word tells us that once we've been forgiven by God, our sins are gone, and He will never bring them back up to us again.

God Promises To Forgive Us and Cleanse Us

The apostle John also shared a major insight on forgiveness in First John 1:9. He said, "If we confess our sins, he [God] is faithful and just to forgive us our sins, and to cleanse us from all unrighteousness." The word "confess" is a translation of the Greek word *homologeo*, which means *to agree, affirm, confess,* or *profess*. It can also mean *to say the same thing* or *to be in alignment with another's thoughts and words*.

To confess your sins to God means you are calling sin what He calls sin in your life; you are in alignment with His thoughts and words about your actions. And by admitting and affirming your wrongs to God, He promises to "forgive" you. This word "forgive" is again the Greek word *aphesis*, from the word *aphiemi*, meaning *to permanently dismiss*, *release*, and *let go*, and *never bring it up again*.

In addition to canceling our debt of sin, God also vows "…to cleanse us from all unrighteousness" (1 John 1:9). The word "cleanse" here is the Greek word *katharidzo*, from the word *katharos*, which means *to clean*, and describes something that is *purged*, *pure*, or *unstained*. Hence, it is *guiltless*, *innocent*, and *upright*. The blood of Jesus does such a thorough job of cleansing that we're made pure, upright, and guiltless. By the time God is finished with us, we are spot free and cleansed from all unrighteousness.

Even the word "from" is important. It is the Greek word *apo*, which is a preposition that means *from*, as *away from*, and carries the idea of *separation*. The use of this word lets us know that not only does God cleanse us, but He also *separates* us from our unrighteousness. He no longer identifies us with what we once were or what we once did. Instead, He separates us from that and gives us a brand-new identity. John goes on to say, "I write unto you, little children, because your sins are forgiven you for his name's sake" (1 John 2:12).

The writer of Hebrews takes the topic of forgiveness even further declaring, "How much more shall the blood of Christ, who through the eternal

Spirit offered himself without spot to God, purge your conscience from dead works to serve the living God?" (Hebrews 9:14) In this verse, the word "conscience" is the Greek word *suneidesis*, which describes *inward thoughts, one's self-consideration*, or *self-judgment*. Essentially, John is telling his readers — which includes us — we are so thoroughly cleansed and released by the blood of Jesus that inwardly we should no longer consider ourselves guilty. We have been totally forgiven in Christ!

In our final lesson, we will turn our attention to the last statement of faith in The Apostles' Creed: I believe in…the resurrection of the body, and life everlasting.

STUDY QUESTIONS

Study to shew thyself approved unto God, a workman that needeth not to be ashamed, rightly dividing the word of truth.
— 2 Timothy 2:15

1. In addition to God's indescribable forgiveness, Jesus' death, burial, and resurrection provide us with many other amazing blessings. Carefully read these New Testament passages and identify some of the additional benefits that are yours through the finished work of Christ.

   - Romans 5:10,11 and 2 Corinthians 5:17-19
   - Galatians 3:13,14
   - John 14:27; Colossians 3:15
   - 1 Peter 2:24 (also Isaiah 53:5)
   - 1 Thessalonians 1:10; 5:9,10; Romans 5:9

2. Take time to carefully reflect on Jesus' words in John 3:16-18. What stands out to you from this passage about the motivation of God's heart in sending us Jesus?

3. The blood of Jesus — the total surrender and ultimate sacrifice of His life — is what provides us forgiveness of sins and reconnects us in relationship with God. How important is blood? Consider these key scriptures and jot down what the Holy Spirit reveals to you.

   - Leviticus 17:11
   - Hebrews 9:22

- Hebrews 10:19-22

How is Jesus' blood different than that of animals? (*See* Hebrews 9:11-14; 10:4; and First John 1:7,9.)

PRACTICAL APPLICATION

> But be ye doers of the word, and not hearers only, deceiving your own selves.
> —James 1:22

1. What new aspects of *forgiveness* did you discover in this lesson? How about *repentance* and the *cleansing* God promises? How does it change your view of guilt and condemnation?
2. How do you view yourself when you sin? What difference does it make to you to know that every trace of sin has been completely removed from you once you repent?
3. What parts of this lesson challenged you most? Invite the Holy Spirit to help you to receive God's forgiveness and extend it to others (*see* Ephesians 4:32; Colossians 3:13; Matthew 6:14,15).

LESSON 15

TOPIC

The Resurrection of the Body and Life Everlasting

SCRIPTURES

1. **John 11:25** — Jesus said unto her, I am the resurrection, and the life: he that believeth in me, though he were dead, yet shall he live.
2. **1 Corinthians 15:19,20** — If in this life only we have hope in Christ, we are of all men most miserable. But now is Christ risen from the dead, and become the firstfruits of them that slept.
3. **John 5:28,29** — …The hour is coming, in the which all that are in the graves shall hear his voice, and shall come forth; they that have done good, unto the resurrection of life; and they that have done evil, unto the resurrection of damnation.

4. **1 Thessalonians 4:14-18** — For if we believe that Jesus died and rose again, even so them also which sleep in Jesus will God bring with him. For this we say unto you by the word of the Lord, that we which are alive and remain unto the coming of the Lord shall not prevent them which are asleep. For the Lord himself shall descend from heaven with a shout, with the voice of the archangel, and with the trump of God: and the dead in Christ shall rise first: then we which are alive and remain shall be caught up together with them in the clouds, to meet the Lord in the air: and so shall we ever be with the Lord. Wherefore comfort one another with these words.
5. **1 Corinthians 15:51-53 (*NKJV*)** — Behold, I tell you a mystery: We shall not all sleep, but we shall all be changed — in a moment, in the twinkling of an eye, at the last trumpet. For the trumpet will sound, and the dead will be raised incorruptible, and we shall be changed. For this corruptible must put on incorruption, and this mortal must put on immortality.
6. **Philippians 3:20,21 (*NKJV*)** — For our citizenship is in heaven, from which we also eagerly wait for the Savior, the Lord Jesus Christ, who will transform our lowly body that it may be conformed to His glorious body, according to the working by which He is able even to subdue all things to Himself.
7. **Revelation 20:4,5** — And I saw thrones, and they sat upon them, and judgment was given unto them: and I saw the souls of them that were beheaded for the witness of Jesus, and for the word of God, and which had not worshipped the beast, neither his image, neither had received his mark upon their foreheads, or in their hands; and they lived and reigned with Christ a thousand years. But the rest of the dead lived not again until the thousand years were finished. This is the first resurrection.
8. **Revelation 20:12-15** — And I saw the dead, small and great, stand before God; and the books were opened: and another book was opened, which is the book of life: and the dead were judged out of those things which were written in the books, according to their works. And the sea gave up the dead which were in it; and death and hell delivered up the dead which were in them: and they were judged every man according to their works. And death and hell were cast into the lake of fire. This is the second death. And whosoever was not found written in the book of life was cast into the lake of fire.

GREEK WORDS

1. Amen — ἀμήν (*amen*): amen; an emphasis marker used to emphasize a statement of great importance

SYNOPSIS

The Bible says, "And as it is appointed unto man once to die, but after this the judgment" (Hebrews 9:27). As difficult as it may be to think about, there is a funeral in everyone's future if Jesus doesn't come back first. Coming to this realization earlier in life helps us to live *on purpose* and make the most of every opportunity God places in front of us (*see* Ephesians 5:15-17).

The emphasis of this lesson:

The Bible talks about three different resurrections that are going to take place in the future. There are two resurrections for believers; one resurrection will happen simultaneously with the rapture of the Church, and the other will occur at the end of the Tribulation. Jesus called the third and final resurrection the 'resurrection of damnation,' which is when all who are unsaved will stand before God and give an account for their lives.

A Final Review of The Apostles' Creed

The Apostles' Creed is one of the oldest documents in Christian history. The first form was known as The Old Roman Creed, and it was written in about 140 AD. The version we're using today was written in 390 AD. Interestingly, the word "creed" literally means *I believe*. Thus, The Apostles' Creed is an affirmation of what we as Christians believe. The Early Church called it "the rule of faith," as it is a condensed compilation of the teaching of the apostles. From that time until now, it has served as a "truth filter," helping believers determine what is and isn't authentic Christian teaching. Today, churches all over the world quote The Apostles' Creed as a regular part of their worship service. Here again is The Apostles' Creed:

I believe in God, the Father Almighty,
the Creator of heaven and earth,
and in Jesus Christ, His only Son, our Lord:
Who was conceived of the Holy Spirit,

> born of the Virgin Mary,
> suffered under Pontius Pilate,
> was crucified, died, and was buried.
> He descended into hell.
> The third day He arose again from the dead.
> He ascended into heaven
> and sits at the right hand of God the Father Almighty,
> whence He shall come to judge the living and the dead.
> I believe in the Holy Spirit,
> the holy catholic [universal] church,
> the communion of saints,
> the forgiveness of sins,
> the resurrection of the body,
> and life everlasting. Amen.

Although some recite this creed by rote as merely a religious exercise, others say it from their heart. What we put into it is what we get out of it. When we quote The Apostles' Creed in faith, it is quite powerful and has a way of uniting us with people from all different backgrounds to declare the core beliefs of the Christian faith with one voice. In this lesson, we'll focus on the creed's final statement of faith: "I believe in… the resurrection of the body, and life everlasting."

People Handle Death in Different Ways

Unless we are raptured by Jesus when He comes to snatch His bride away, we all stand a one-in-one chance of going into eternity by way of the grave. It's a statistic that hasn't budged — nor ever will. But the way each of us handles death is a different story. People who believe in God and people without faith react very differently to losing a loved one. A great example of this is found in the humorous but sobering account Rick shared from the early years of his life:

> When I turned 12 years old, I received my social security card, and my daddy said, "Son, if you're old enough to have a social security card, you're old enough to get a job."

I said, "Daddy, I'm only 12 years old. Where am I going to get a job?"

"Well, jump on your bicycle," he said, "Ride over to the cemetery, and ask the director there for a job."

You want me to work in the cemetery? I thought. Nevertheless, as strange as it sounded, I did what my daddy told me. I rode to the cemetery, which was just a few blocks away, and asked to speak with the director.

"My name is Ricky Renner," I said confidently, "And I'm looking for a job."

Much to my surprise, he hired me on the spot, and at 12 years of age, I started doing all sorts of jobs at the cemetery. I mowed the lawn, edged the tombstones, and helped dig the graves. I even assisted in burying the dead. Through it all, I learned a great deal about people's responses to death. Overall, I saw that death was quite tragic for people without faith. In contrast, people who had faith were both positive and hopeful.

Years later, when I was being trained in ministry, my first assignment from my pastor was to conduct a funeral for an unsaved man. His family was also unsaved. I can still vividly remember the crushing weight of grief that lay heavy on the people that came into the parlor. At the end of the service, they opened the casket so the family could walk by and pay their last respects to the deceased. When I saw the man's unsaved elderly mother approach the coffin, the hopelessness on her face was overwhelming.

As I continued to watch, this devastated, grief-stricken woman did something that took all of us off guard. Before we knew it, she had climbed up inside the casket and was clinging to her dead son, weeping uncontrollably. Then in great desperation, she began pounding her fists on her deceased son's chest, shouting, "Speak to me! Speak to me, son!" She just couldn't deal with the sudden termination of his life.

When believers lost a loved one, the funeral services were quite different. I remember when my father died, and I was looking at his body in the casket. Although I deeply loved him, I was not gripped with a sense of overwhelming sorrow because I knew what the Bible says about those who die in Christ. First, I knew that the body lying in the casket was not my father — it was just the human shell he had lived in during his lifetime. And according to Second Corinthians 5:6-8, his soul and spirit were already in the presence of the Lord.

So, as I stood there, I thought, *This is the last time I'll see my father's body like this. The next time I see him, he's going to be completely different and so wonderful!* I knew that I knew that although my father's body had been sown in weakness, as the Bible says, he would be raised in power in the resurrection (*see* 1 Corinthians 15:43).

The resurrection of the dead is an amazing truth that is foundational to our faith. Indeed, our faith is securely rooted in this firm belief. First Corinthians 15:26 says death is definitely an enemy. But according to First Corinthians 15:54 and 55, Christ's resurrection and our own future resurrection remove the sting out of death, and it is not something we need to fear.

Jesus Taught About the Resurrection

Jesus made a powerful declaration in John 11:25. He said, "…I am the resurrection, and the life: he that believeth in me, though he were dead, yet shall he live." Jesus is the Resurrection and the Life! He has all power over death, hell, and the grave, and one day everyone who has died will be resurrected.

How important is having faith in the resurrection? The apostle Paul said, "If in this life only we have hope in Christ, we are of all men most miserable. But now is Christ risen from the dead, and become the firstfruits of them that slept" (1 Corinthians 15:19,20). In this passage, Paul categorically stated that Jesus' resurrection from the dead is the guarantee that we also will be raised from the dead. Christ was the *firstfruits*, which means His resurrection is the promise that another harvest of resurrections will follow after Him.

Jesus refers to two resurrections in John 5:28,29. He said, "…The hour is coming, in the which all that are in the graves shall hear his voice, and shall come forth; they that have done good, unto the resurrection of life; and they that have done evil, unto the resurrection of damnation." Here from Jesus' own lips, we learn that there's going to be a resurrection for those who are righteous — in other words, for those who are saved by their faith in the redemptive work of Jesus.

Additionally, Jesus said there's also going to be another resurrection that will occur for those who have done evil. He called it "the resurrection of damnation." This will be a resurrection of those who rejected Christ and wanted nothing to do with His offer of salvation. When will these future resurrections take place?

The Resurrection of the Saved Happens First

Everyone who has died in Christ will be raised from the dead at the moment of the Rapture. This is the resurrection of the saved, and it is what the Bible calls *the first resurrection*. It will happen in the very near future when Jesus comes for the Church. If we have already died, we will be raised from the dead to meet the Lord first in the air. The apostle Paul gives us the details of this resurrection in First Thessalonians 4:14-17:

> **For if we believe that Jesus died and rose again, even so them also which sleep in Jesus will God bring with him.**
>
> **For this we say unto you by the word of the Lord, that we which are alive and remain unto the coming of the Lord shall not prevent them which are asleep.**
>
> **For the Lord himself shall descend from heaven with a shout, with the voice of the archangel, and with the trump of God: and the dead in Christ shall rise first:**
>
> **Then we which are alive and remain shall be caught up together with them in the clouds, to meet the Lord in the air: and so shall we ever be with the Lord.**

When Paul wrote of those who "sleep in Jesus," he was referring to Christians who have already died. The souls and spirits of these saints who've gone to Heaven before us will come back with Jesus at the time of the Rapture. Their bodies will be supernaturally resurrected back to life and instantly reunited with their soul and spirit. That's what verse 16 declares: "…The dead in Christ shall rise *first*." The word "first" is the Greek word *proton*, which means *first in sequence* or *first in the order of priority*.

Before anything else takes place, Christians who have died will be raised back to life. Again, this is *the first resurrection*. Then all the believers that are still alive and awaiting Christ's return will be caught up to meet the Lord in the air, and forever we will all be with Him! Paul finishes this chapter with these instructions: "Wherefore comfort one another with these words" (1 Thessalonians 4:18).

The Rapture is a mystery. First Corinthians 15:51-53 (*NKJV*) says, "Behold, I tell you a mystery: We shall not all sleep, but we shall all be changed — in a moment, in the twinkling of an eye, at the last trumpet. For the trumpet will sound, and the dead will be raised incorruptible, and we shall be changed. For this corruptible must put on incorruption, and this mortal must put on immortality."

Paul also talked about the transformation of our bodies in Philippians 3:20,21 (*NKJV*) where he said, "For our citizenship is in heaven, from which we also eagerly wait for the Savior, the Lord Jesus Christ, who will transform our lowly body that it may be conformed to His glorious body, according to the working by which He is able even to subdue all things to Himself."

What a day it will be when those who have died in Christ will have their dead, corruptible bodies miraculously transformed into incorruptible ones! And we who are alive and mortal — in the twinkling of an eye — will change and put on immortality. That marvelous day is fast approaching.

There's a Second Resurrection for the Righteous

Another resurrection for the righteous in Christ will take place *after* the Rapture. This resurrection will occur at the end of the Tribulation, and it will be for those who died as martyrs for their faith in Christ during the Tribulation. In Revelation 20:4 and 5, John wrote:

> **And I saw thrones, and they sat upon them, and judgment was given unto them: and I saw the souls of them that were beheaded for the witness of Jesus, and for the word of God, and which had not worshipped the beast, neither his image, neither had received his mark upon their foreheads, or in their hands; and they lived and reigned with Christ a thousand years. But the rest of the dead lived not again until the thousand years were finished. This is the first resurrection.**

Here we find that those who are martyred for their faith during the Tribulation are going to be raised from the dead at the end of it. So like the saints who will be taken to Heaven in the Rapture, these Tribulation saints will also live and reign with Christ in His Kingdom for a thousand years.

The Third Resurrection Is for the Unrighteous

Notice the Bible says, "But *the rest of the dead* lived not again until the thousand years were finished…" (Revelation 20:5). Therefore, there is a certain group of people that will remain in the grave until after the Millennial (1,000-year) reign of Christ. These are the unrighteous — those who never received Jesus as their Savior and Lord.

Thus, the final resurrection of the dead will be for sinners who died in their sins. It's what Jesus called the "resurrection unto damnation." We find this event described in Revelation 20:12-15:

> **And I saw the dead, small and great, stand before God; and the books were opened: and another book was opened, which is the book of life: and the dead were judged out of those things which were written in the books, according to their works.**
>
> **And the sea gave up the dead which were in it; and death and hell delivered up the dead which were in them: and they were judged every man according to their works.**
>
> **And death and hell were cast into the lake of fire. This is the second death.**
>
> **And whosoever was not found written in the book of life was cast into the lake of fire.**

Who are "the rest of the dead" referred to in Revelation 20:5? They are the unrighteous who did not die with faith in Jesus. In this final resurrection, the unsaved will be summoned by God to be judged before the Great White Throne Judgment. The Bible teaches that unsaved people are destined for eternity in hell. Although people don't talk much about hell, Jesus said it exists, and people are going there.

Therefore, it's crucial that we understand there is a future judgment for the unsaved, and because none of us want anyone to experience it and spend eternity in hell, we are to share the saving news of Jesus Christ. It's also our job to pray and ask the Holy Spirit to open the eyes of the spiritually blind so they can come to Christ and avoid this final judgment that will happen at the end of the Millennial reign.

Friend, if Jesus tarries in His coming, there will be a funeral in each of our futures. But if we're believers who die with faith in Christ, we will be resurrected to new life! Jesus was the "firstfruits" and the guarantee that there would be a great harvest of His people resurrected after Him, and the hope of that glorious event that lies ahead in the not-too-distant future includes us! So, there is no need to fear death.

Remember, there are three resurrections that will take place, and regardless of whether people have accepted or rejected Jesus, every person who has ever lived is going to be raised in one of the three resurrections to come. This truth is preserved in The Apostles' Creed, which ends with a hearty "Amen." In Greek, this is an emphasis marker used to emphasize a statement of great importance. So, along with John, we offer our enthusiastic *Amen* and say as He did, "…Even so, come, Lord Jesus!" (Revelation 22:20)

STUDY QUESTIONS

> **Study to shew thyself approved unto God, a workman that needeth not to be ashamed, rightly dividing the word of truth.**
> **— 2 Timothy 2:15**

1. According to Romans 1:2-4, what does Jesus' resurrection from the dead firmly establish?
2. Jesus demonstrated His power over death — even during His earthly ministry. In what specific way did Jesus prove His authority over death in the lives of the people in the following passages?
   - Matthew 9:18-26 (also in Mark 5:22-24 and 35-42)
   - Luke 7:11-17
   - John 11:17-44
3. According to Hebrews 2:14 and 15, how did Jesus effectively deal with the paralyzing fear of death? What does Revelation 1:17 and 18 say Jesus holds in His hand? Why is this significant?
4. Some critics claim that the word "rapture" is not in the Bible, and while that may be true of today's English translations, the imagery of the Rapture is represented in several places. Take a few moments to play detective and uncover the eight different raptures recorded in these passages. What is the Holy Spirit showing you through these multiple examples? *See* Genesis 5:21-24; Second Kings 2:9-12;

Acts 1:4-9 and 8:35-40; Second Corinthians 12:1-6; First Thessalonians 4:15-17; Revelation 4:1,2 and 11:1-12.

PRACTICAL APPLICATION

> But be ye doers of the word, and not hearers only, deceiving your own selves.
> —James 1:22

1. Prior to this lesson, did you know that there was more than one resurrection? How does knowing that there are three resurrections change your view of eternity?
2. Is death something you've feared? If so, was it *before* or *after* you received Christ? How does knowing God's plan for eternity (including the resurrection) change your view of death?
3. What stood out to you in this teaching about the reality of hell for all those who will stand before the Great White Throne Judgment? How did Jesus describe this horrific place in the gospels? (Consider Luke 16:19-31 and Mark 9:43-48.)
4. Who do you know personally that does not yet know Jesus? Does knowing what hell will be like give you a different perspective — maybe even a sense of urgency — about sharing the Gospel with them while there is still time?
5. Ask the Holy Spirit to help you respond with love for these people, not out of panic. Remember, God wants to see them saved infinitely more than you do. Invite the Holy Spirit to show them God's love and to show you how to pray for them and be ready when the opportunity arises to have a meaningful conversation (*see* 1 Peter 3:15).

Notes

Notes

Notes

CLAIM YOUR FREE RESOURCE!

As a way of introducing you further to the teaching ministry of Rick Renner, we would like to send you FREE of charge his teaching, "How To Receive a Miraculous Touch From God" on CD or USB format.

In His earthly ministry, Jesus commonly healed *all* who were sick of *all* their diseases. In this profound message, learn about the manifold dimensions of Christ's wisdom, goodness, power, and love toward all humanity who came to Him in faith with their needs.

☑ YES, I want to receive Rick Renner's monthly teaching letter!

Simply scan the QR code to claim this resource or go to:
renner.org/claim-your-free-offer

WITH US!

renner.org

facebook.com/rickrenner • facebook.com/rennerdenise

youtube.com/rennerministries • youtube.com/deniserenner

instagram.com/rickrrenner • instagram.com/rennerministries_
instagram.com/rennerdenise

www.ingramcontent.com/pod-product-compliance
Lightning Source LLC
Chambersburg PA
CBHW071118090426
42736CB00012B/1943